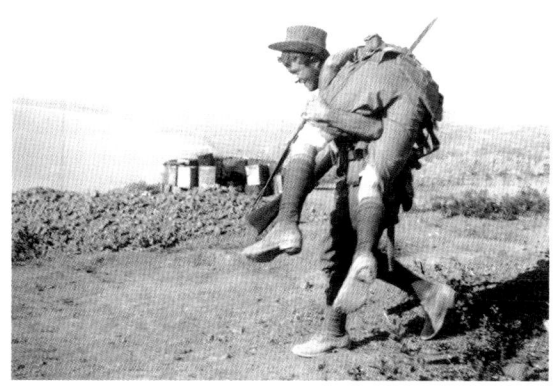

ANZAC
Memories
IMAGES FROM THE GREAT WAR

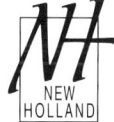

NEW
HOLLAND

compiled by Don Donovan

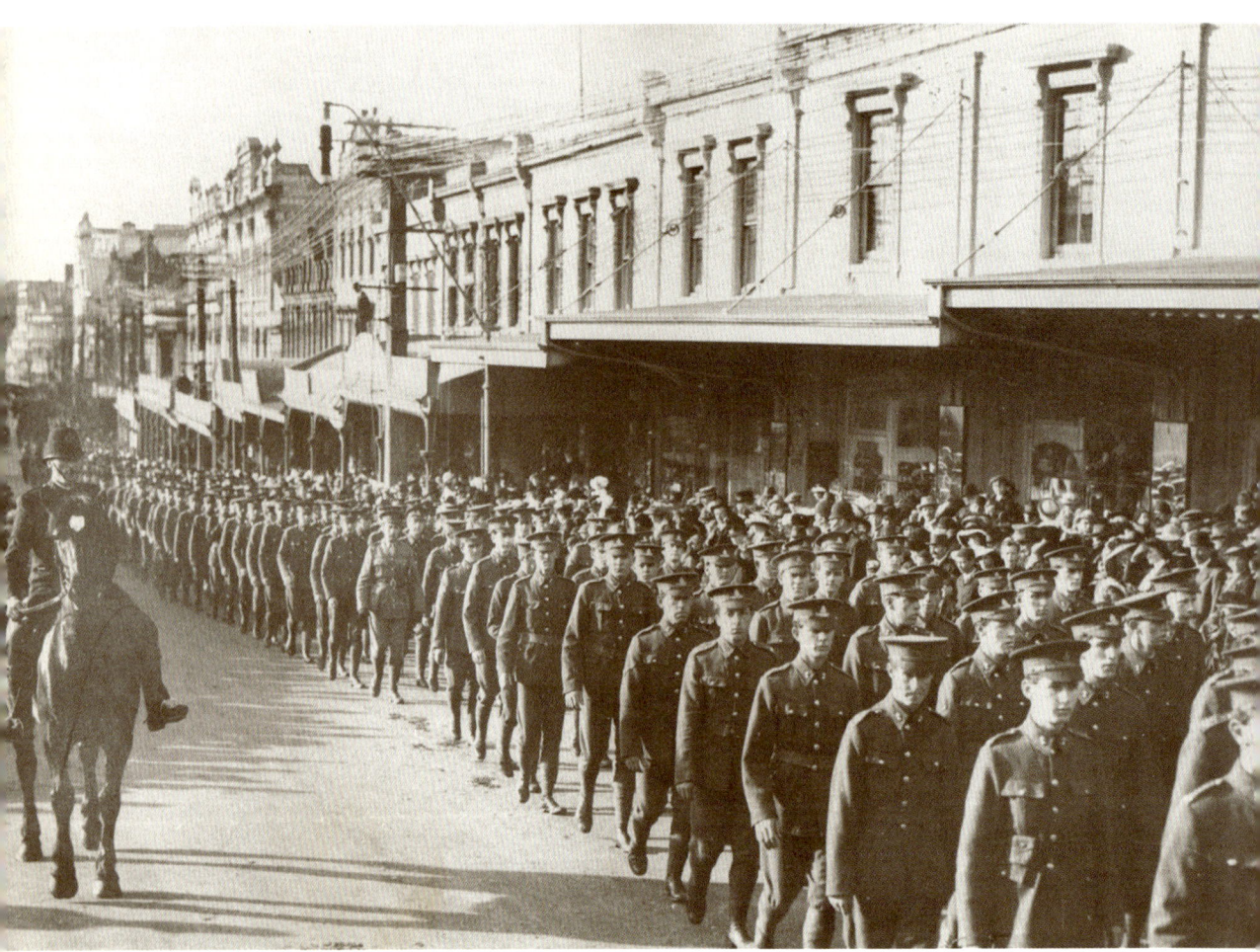

Now, God be thanked Who has matched us with His hour,
And caught our youth, and wakened us from sleeping.

Rupert Brooke

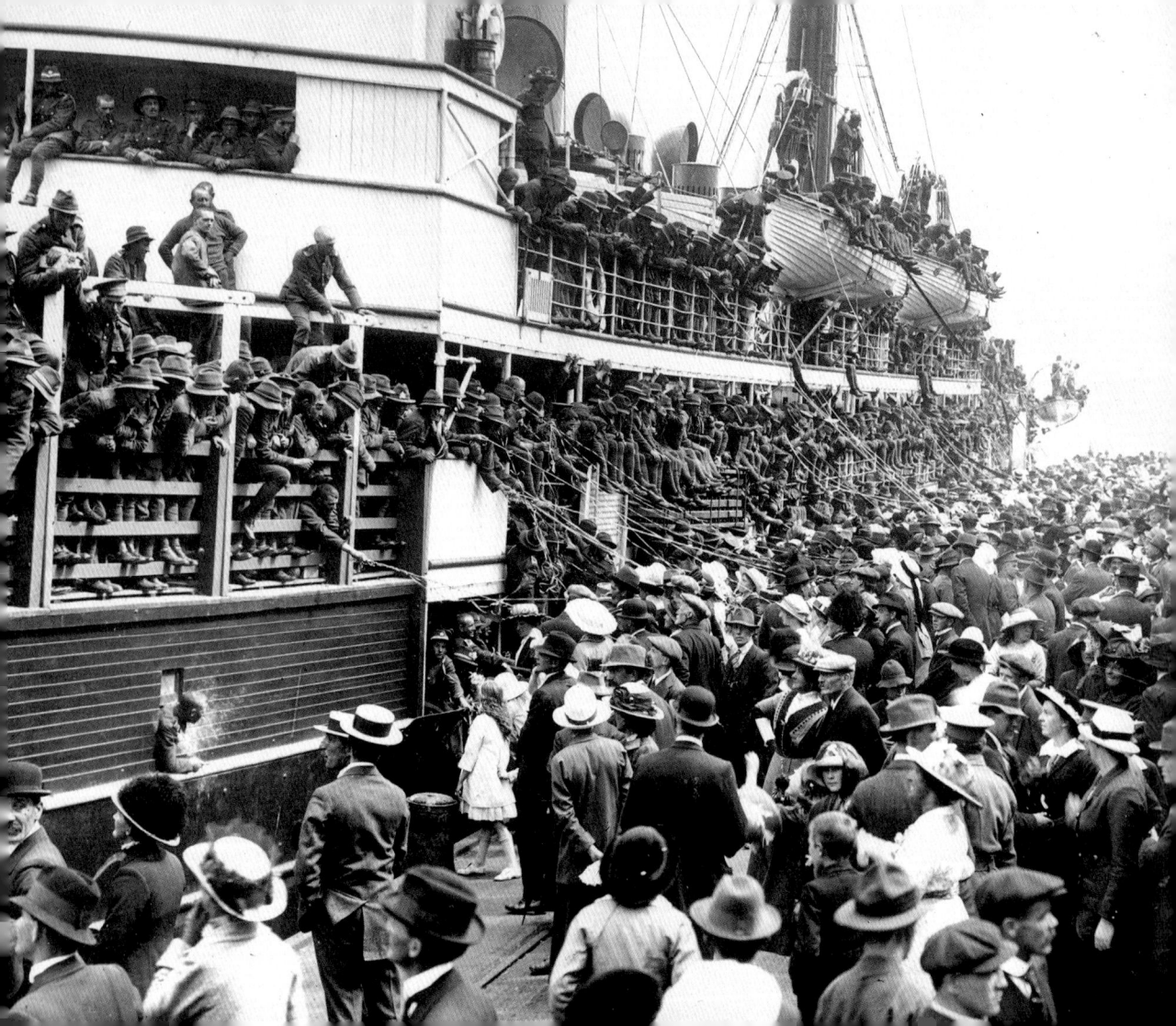

Oh, we don't want to lose you but we think you ought to go.
For your King and your country both need you so.
We shall want you and miss you
But with all our might and main
We shall cheer you, thank you, bless you
When you come home again.

Paul Rubens, Great War Song Lyrics: 'Your King and Country Want You'

A heavily laden troopship leaves for war half a world away

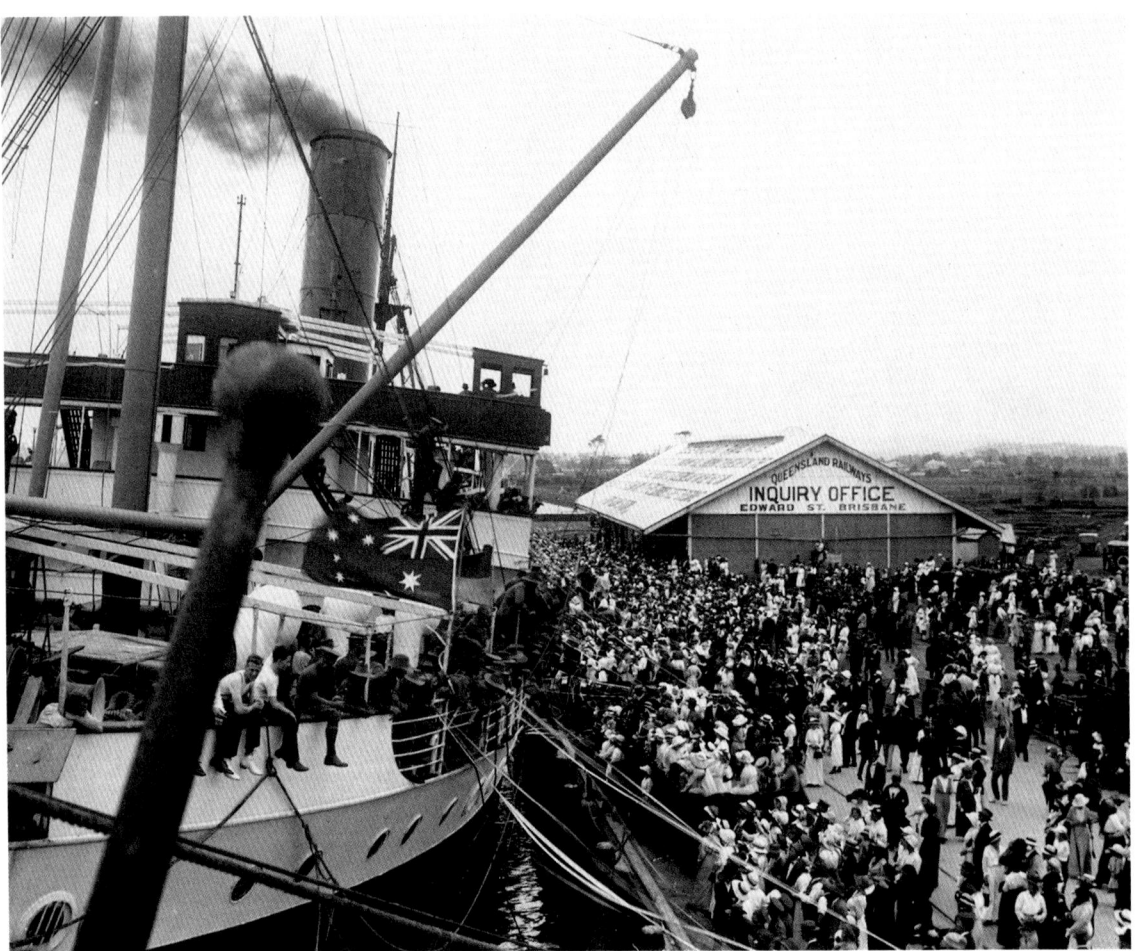

If the Old Country is at war, so are we.

Joseph Cook, Prime Minister of Australia

Carrying reinforcements, a troop transport prepares to sail from Brisbane, 1916
Australian War Museum (negative no. H02242)

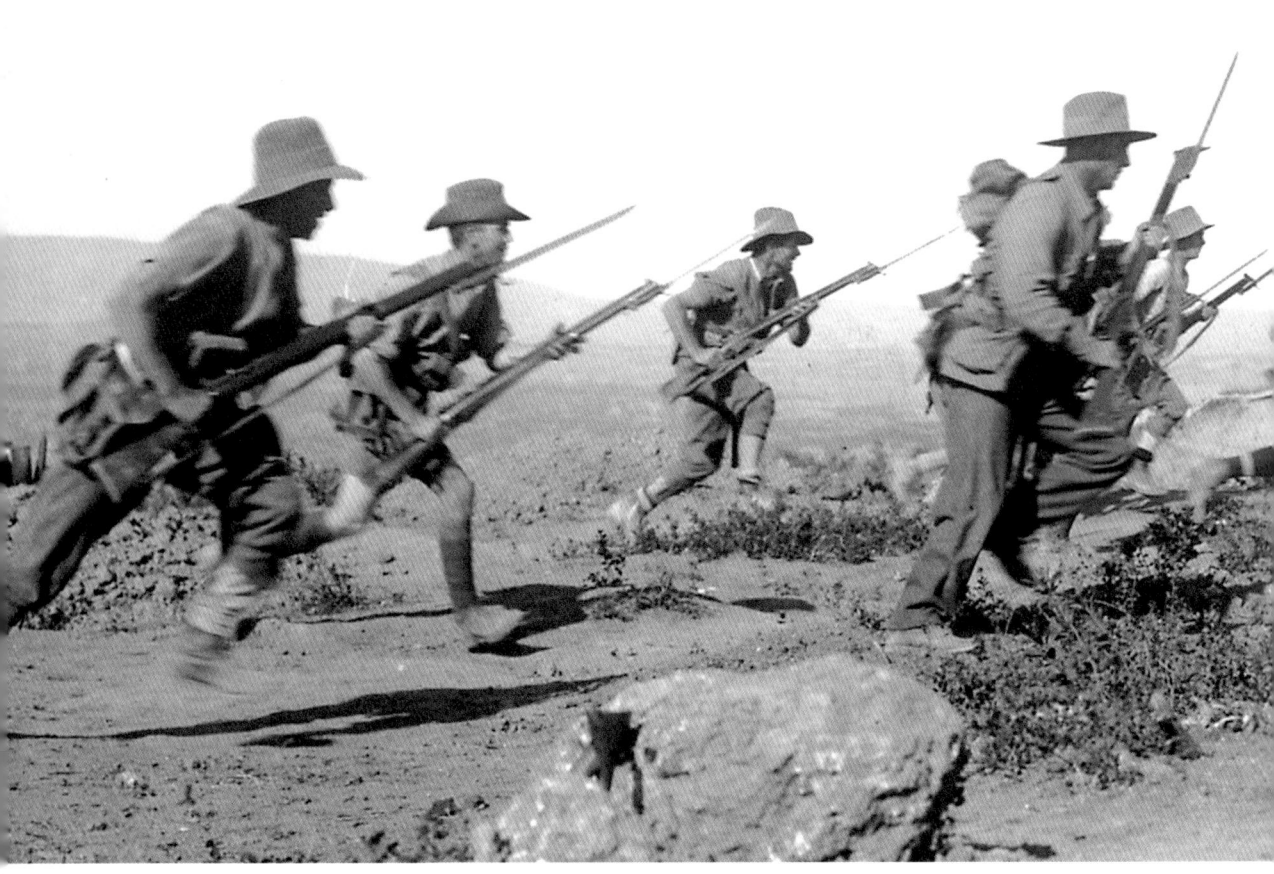

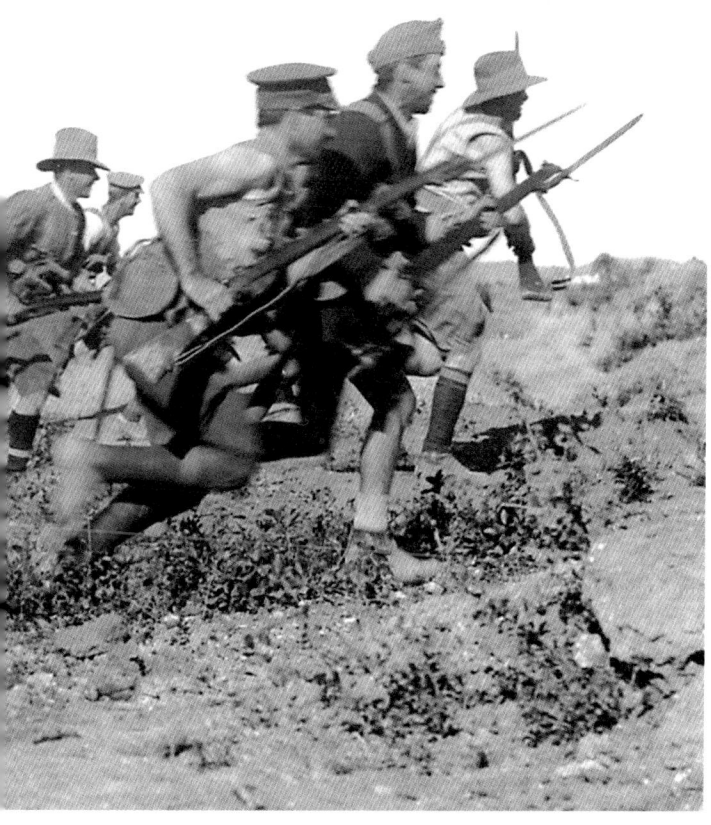

... we were taught the British system ... It consisted in benumbing an enemy with the foulest blows of foot or rifle-butt ... killing him economically with the bayonet ... in a brisk forward motion.

Alexander Craig Aitken

ANZAC troops charge uphill with fixed bayonets, Gallipoli, 1915

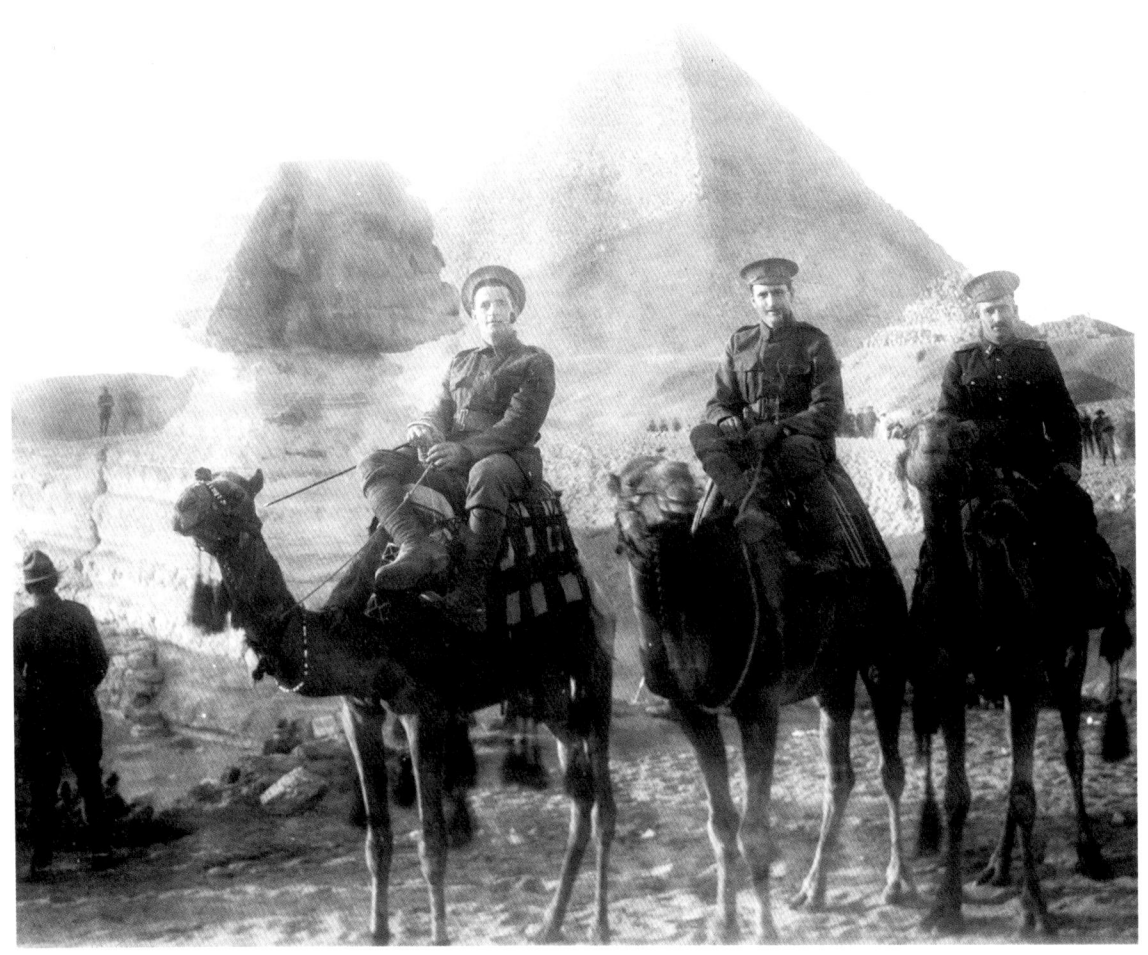

I have not yet been afraid.

Roland Leighton

New Zealand servicemen enjoy unexpected benefits before being sent to the battlefield

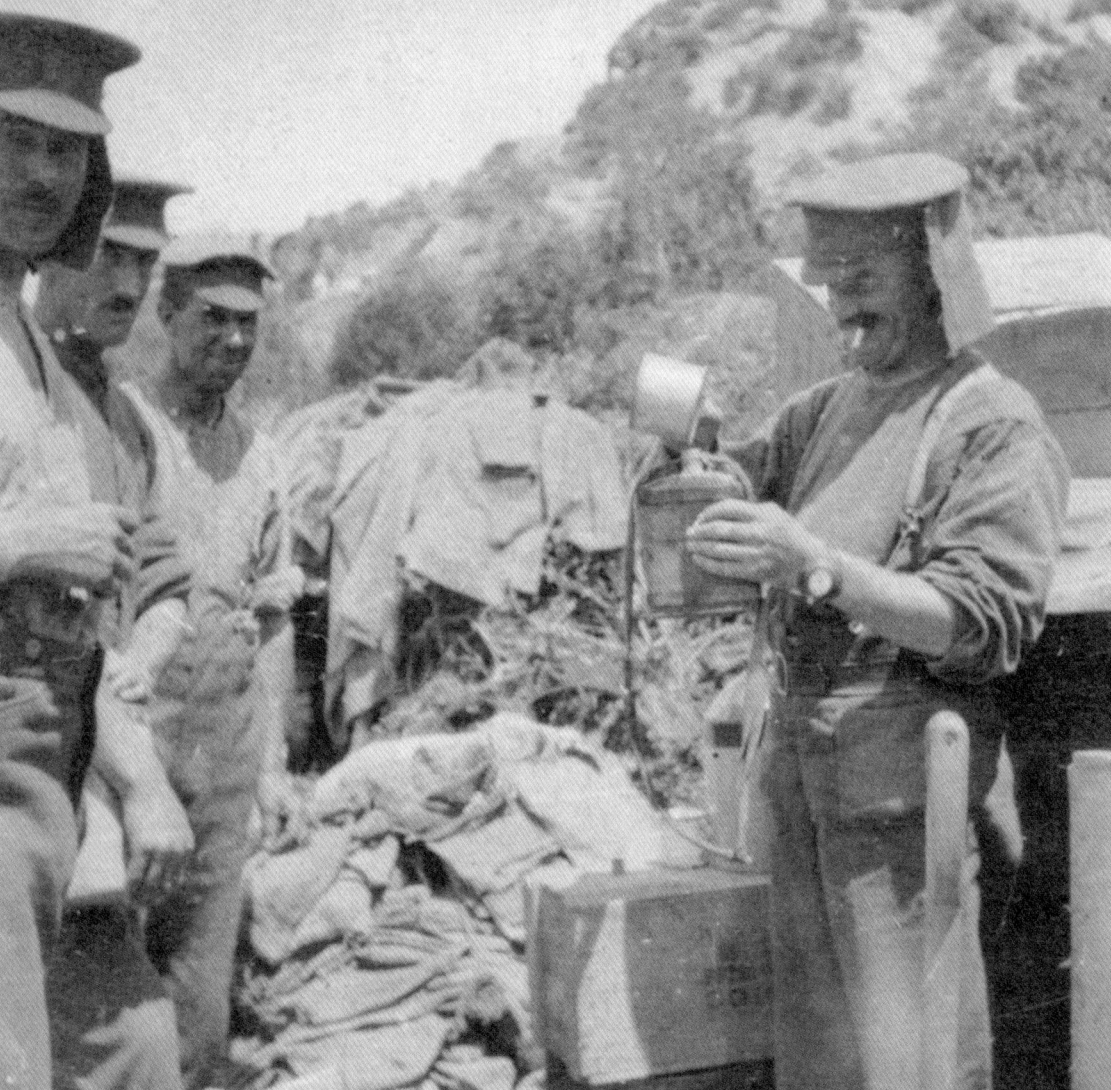

None but a coward dares to boast that he has never known fear.

Ferdinand Foch

The daily ration of rum to keep the spirits up and the fear down
AUCKLAND WAR MEMORIAL MUSEUM (29496)

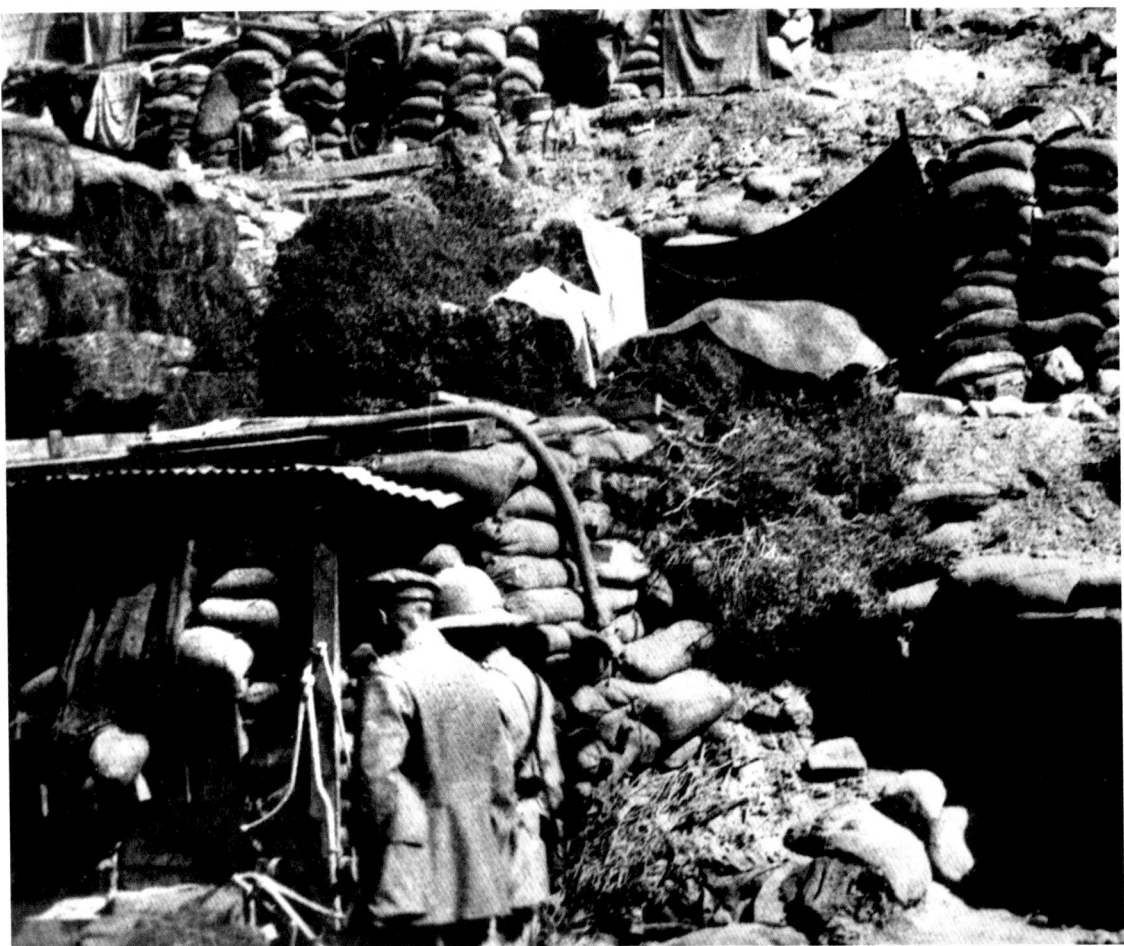

Gallipoli was a bastard of a place. I never understood what we were fighting for. All I could think of was that I never wanted to go back to the bloody place.

Albert White, aged 100, *Sydney Morning Herald*, 17 May 2002

Dugouts on the slopes above the beach at Anzac Cove, Gallipoli, August 1915

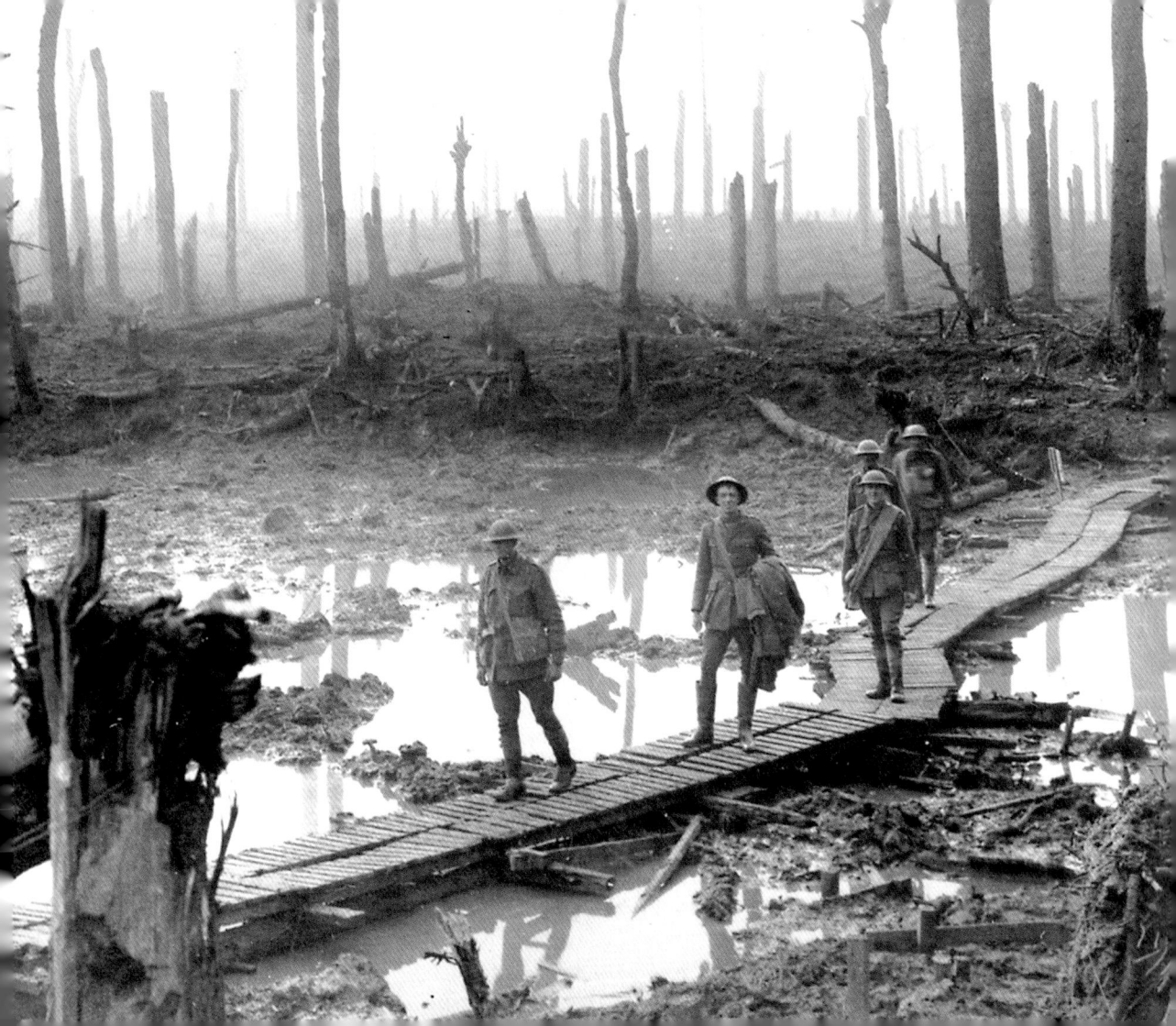

Why did we join the army, boys?
Why did we join the army?
Why did we come to France to fight?
We mus' have been bloody well barmy.

Soldiers' song

Across a morass of flooded shell holes, Australian troops
walk on duckboards near Passchendaele, Belgium, 1917

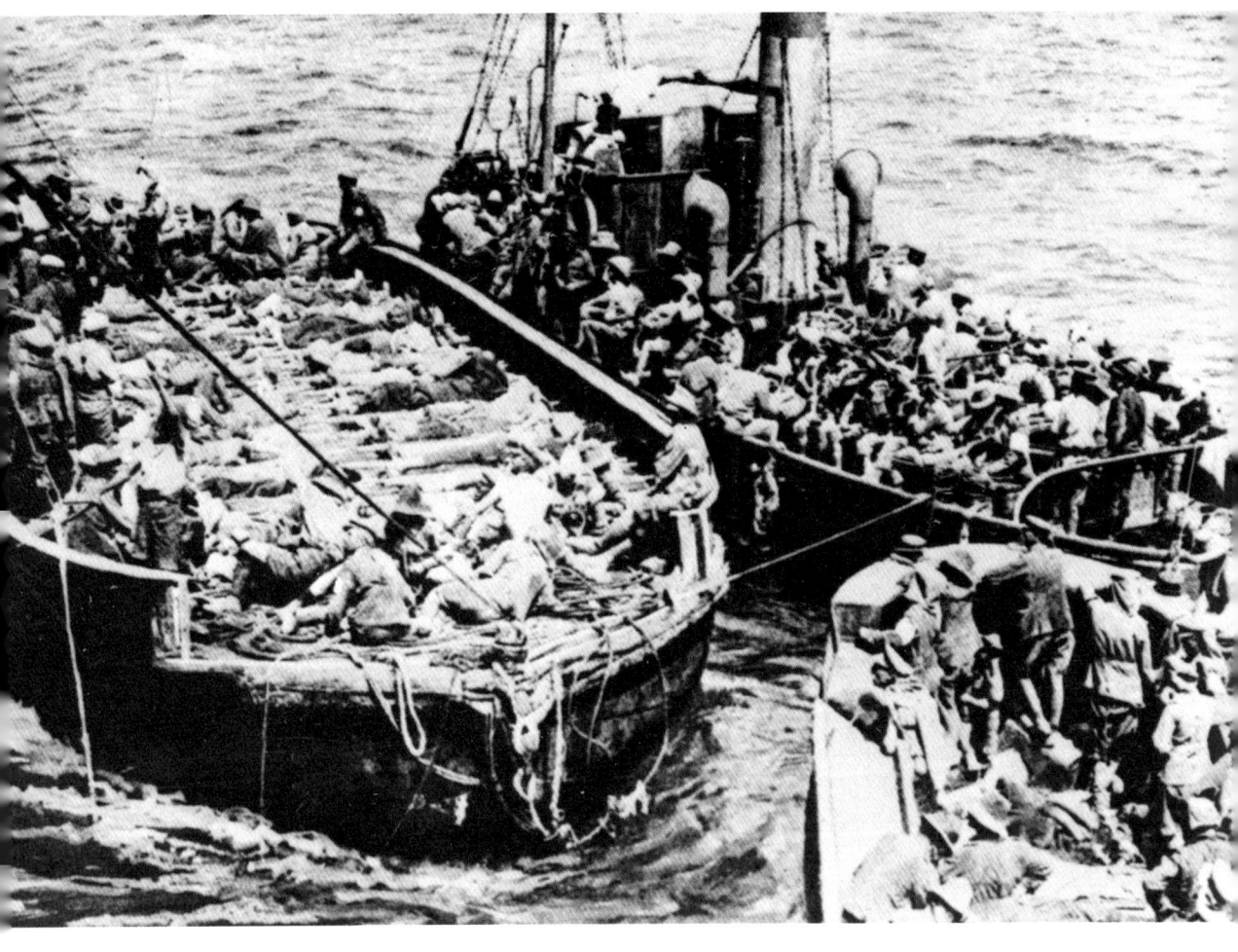

Well done, ANZAC, you are sticking it splendidly.

General Sir Ian Hamilton, Commander, Mediterranean Expeditionary Force, 27 April 1915

Wounded being evacuated by barge from Anzac Cove

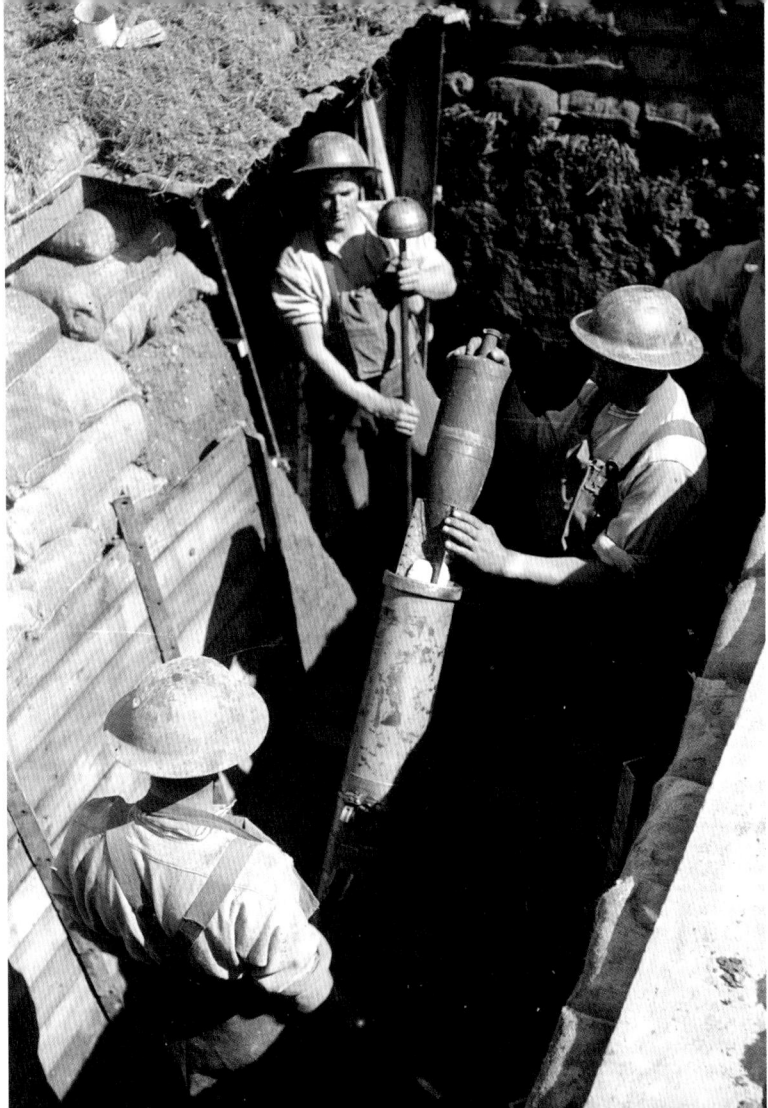

A few honest men are better than numbers.

Oliver Cromwell

New Zealand soldiers loading a trench mortar near Colincamps, France

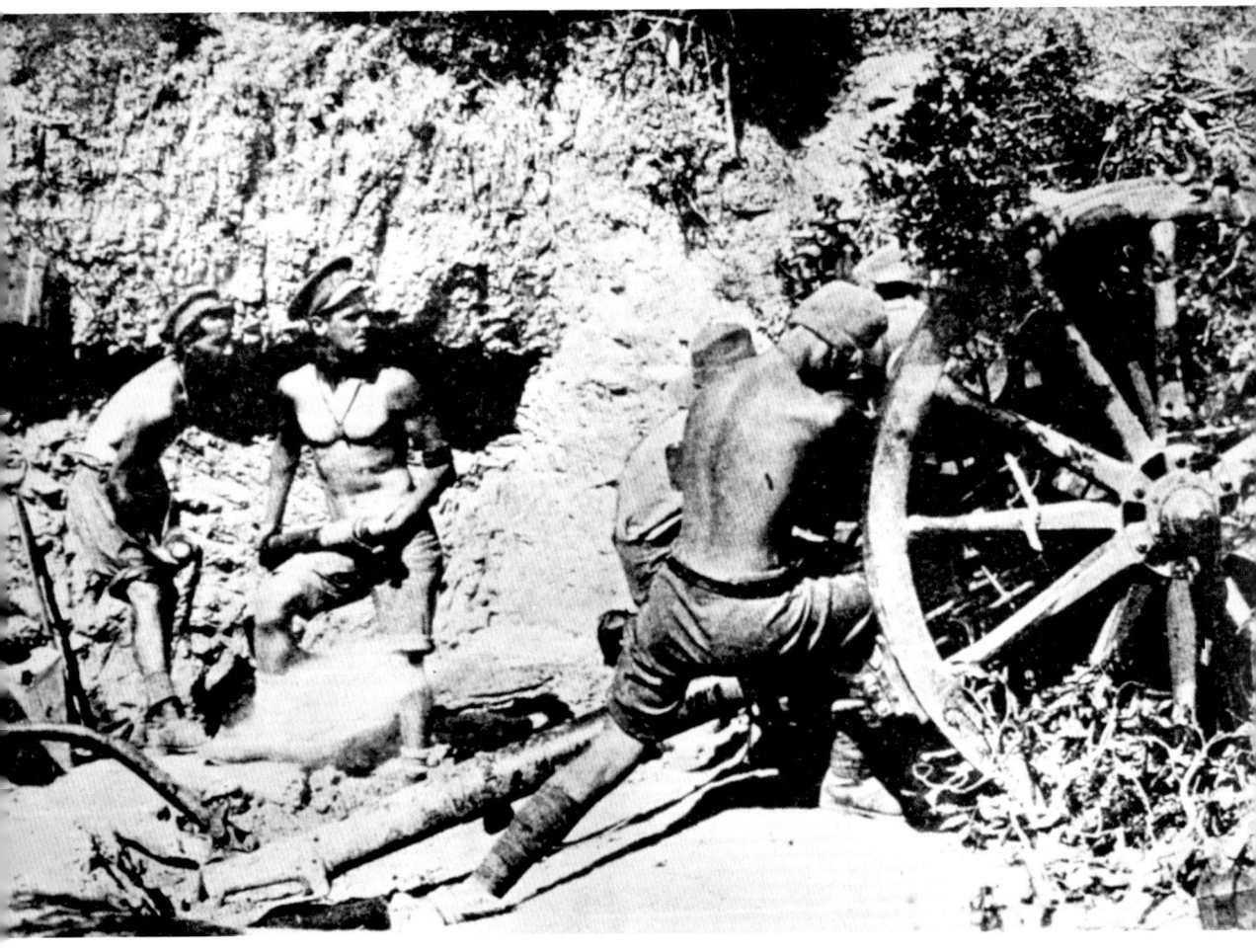

The Guns, Thank God, The Guns ...

Rudyard Kipling

Artillerymen serving a field cannon, Gallipoli

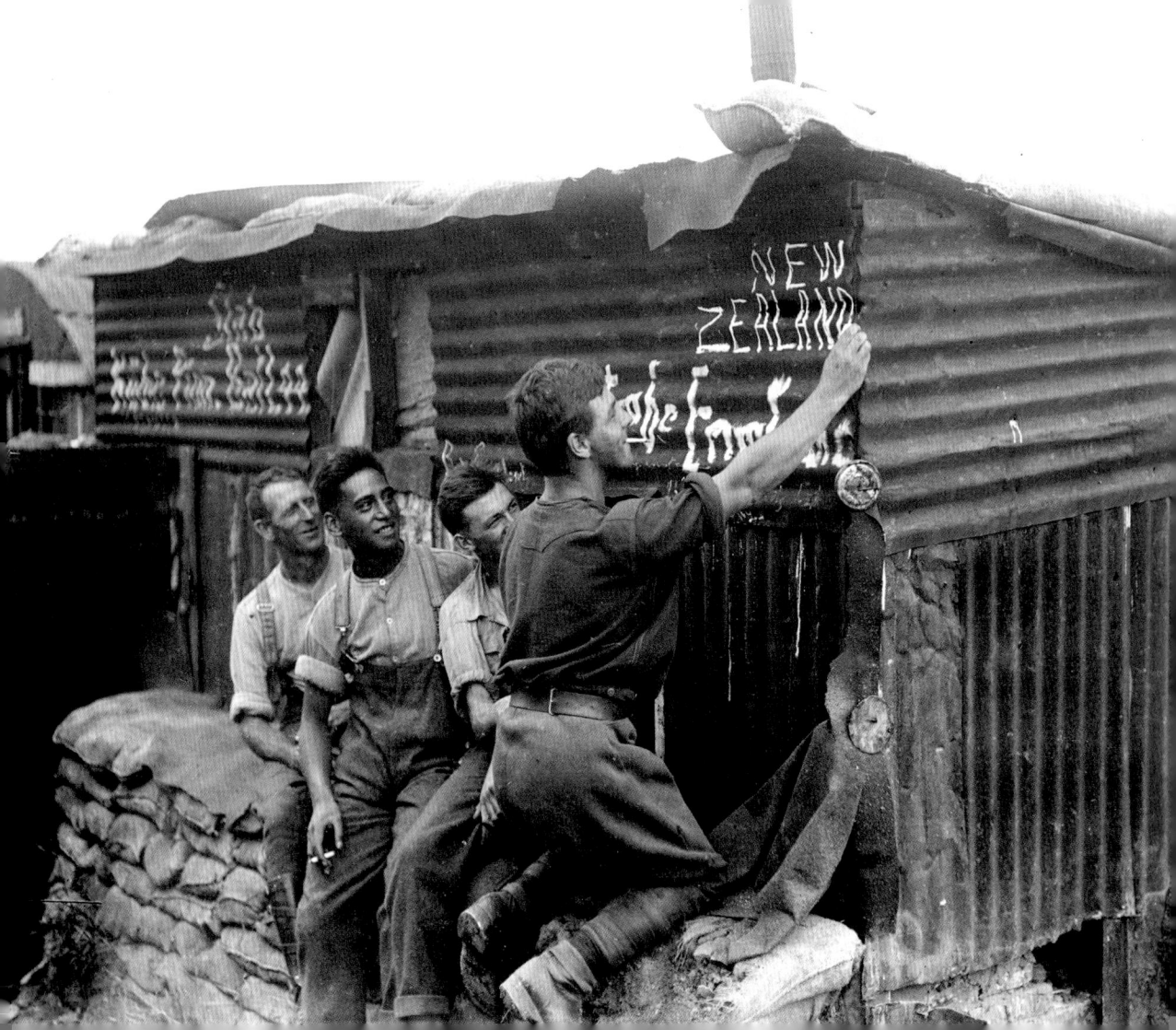

Absence from whom we love is worse than death.

William Cowper

A Kiwi soldier establishes a home from home on the Western Front

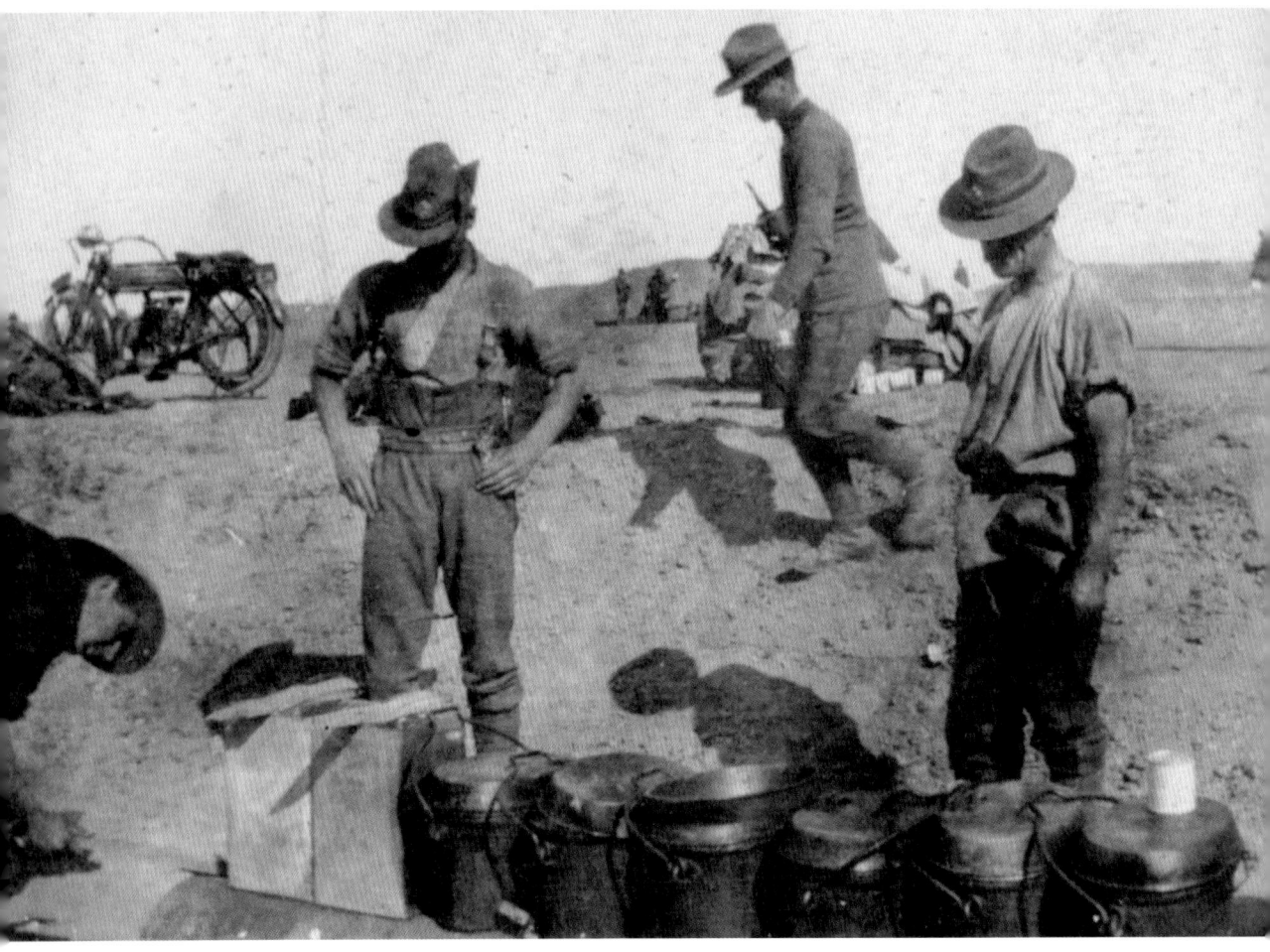

An army marches on its stomach.

Napoleon Bonaparte

Army cooks prepare a meal behind the front line

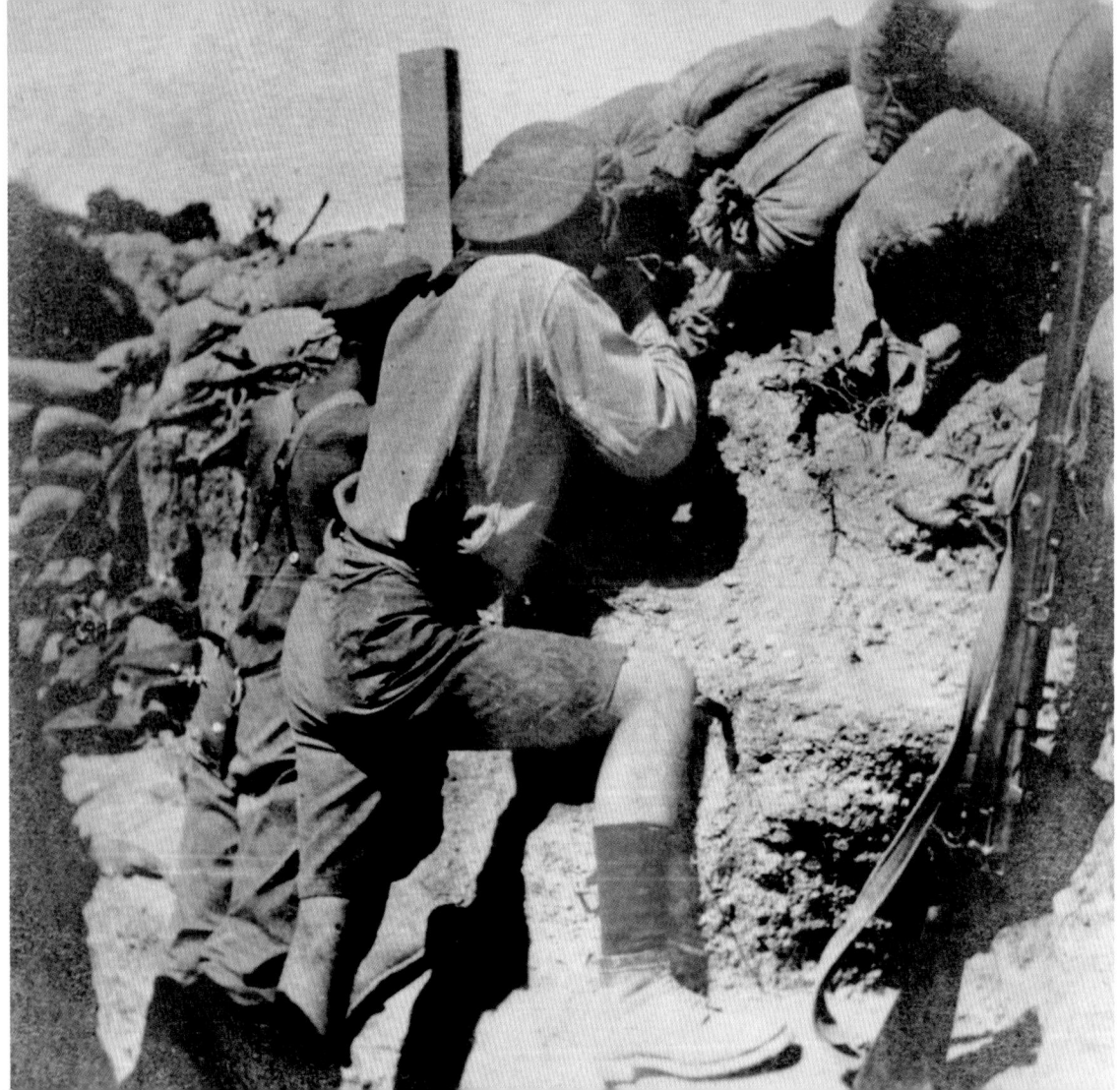

The condition upon which God hath given liberty to man is eternal vigilance ...

John Philpot Curran

Close observation of the enemy by sniper and
periscope from below the parapet of a forward trench

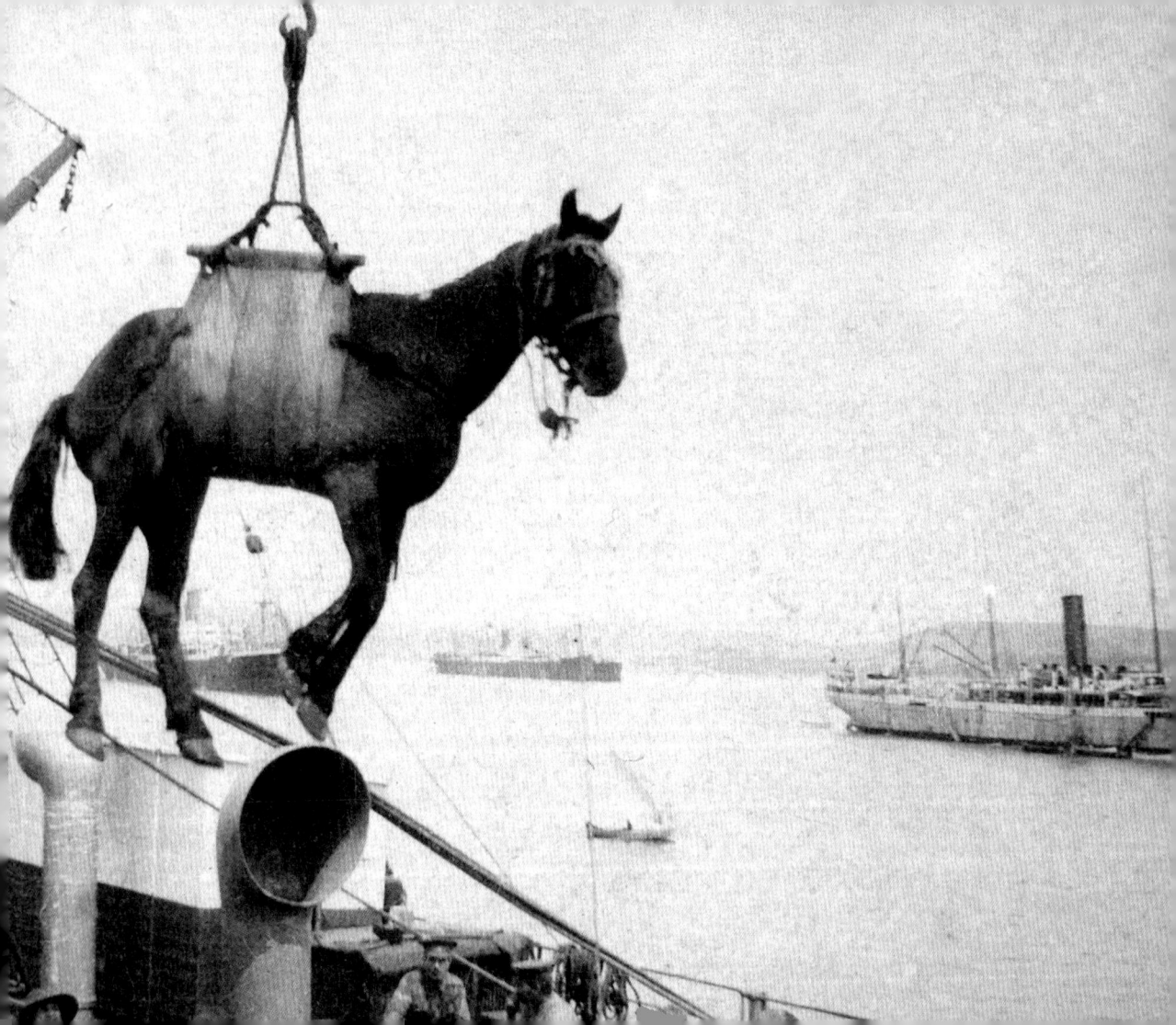

War is a series of catastrophes which result in victory.

Albert Pike

A horse is unloaded from a troop transport ship at Gallipoli, 1915

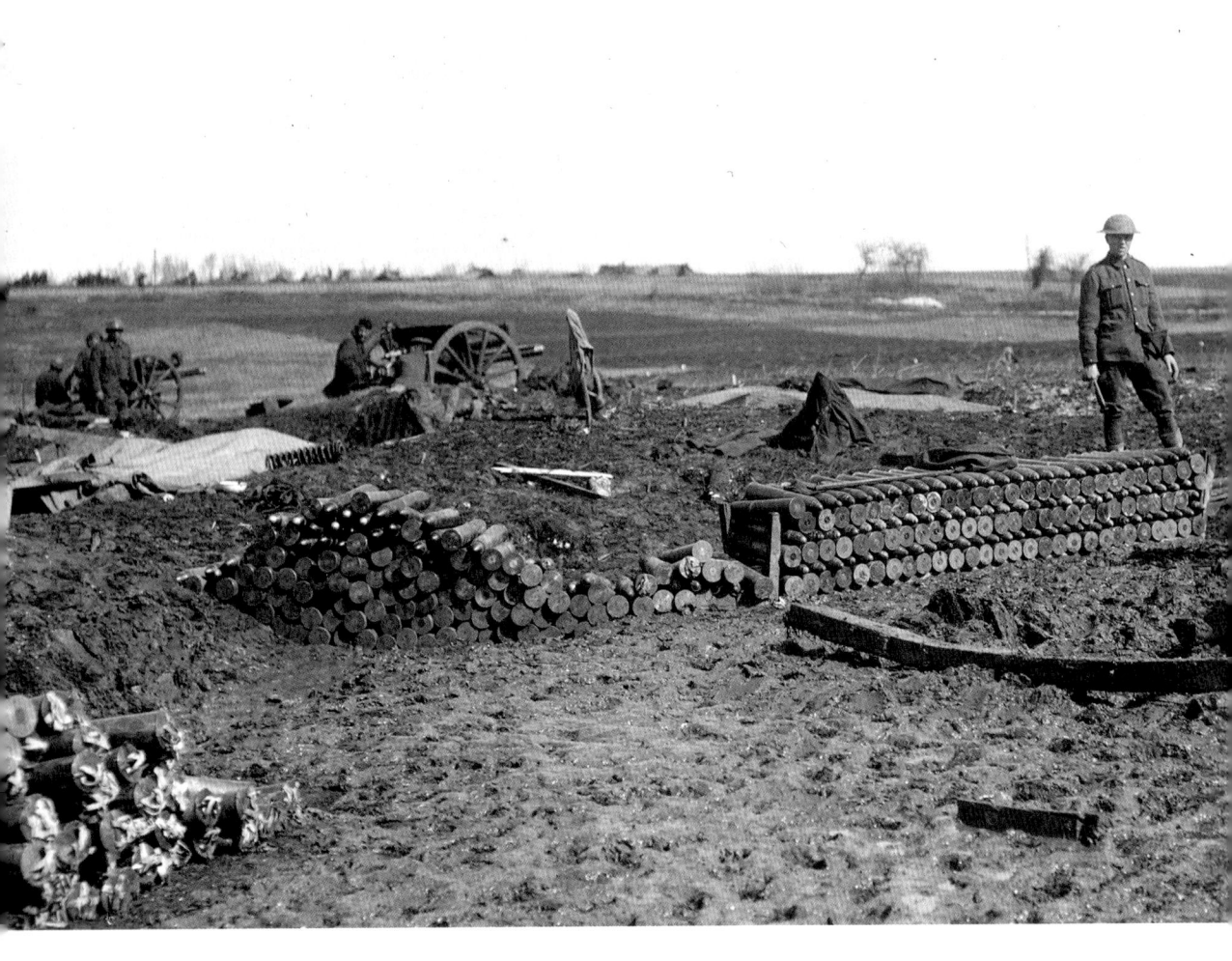

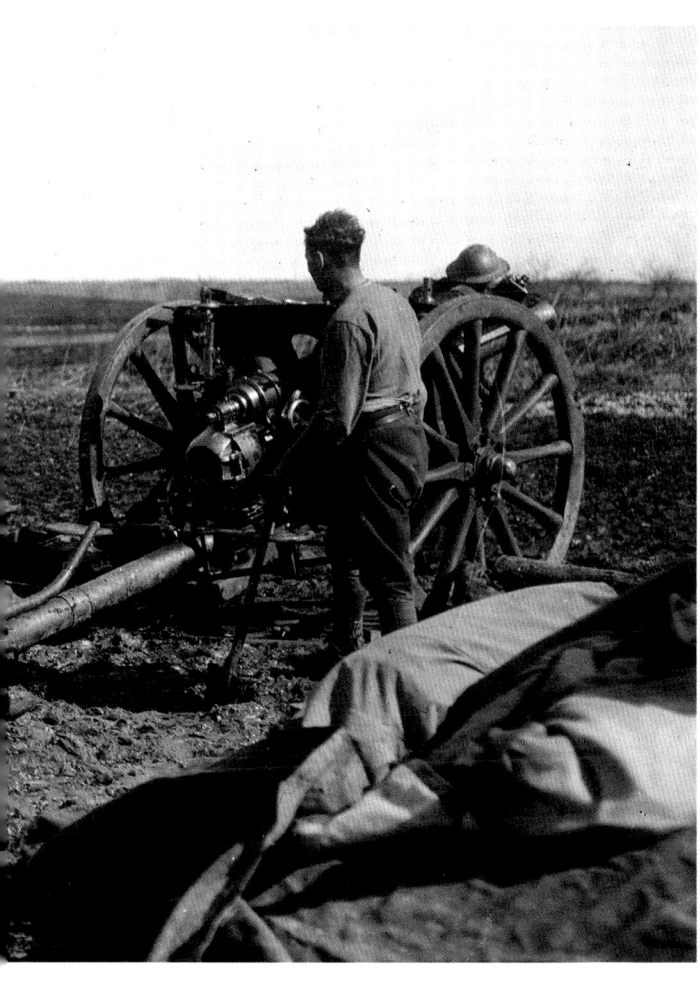

Accurst be he that
first invented war.

Thomas Marlowe

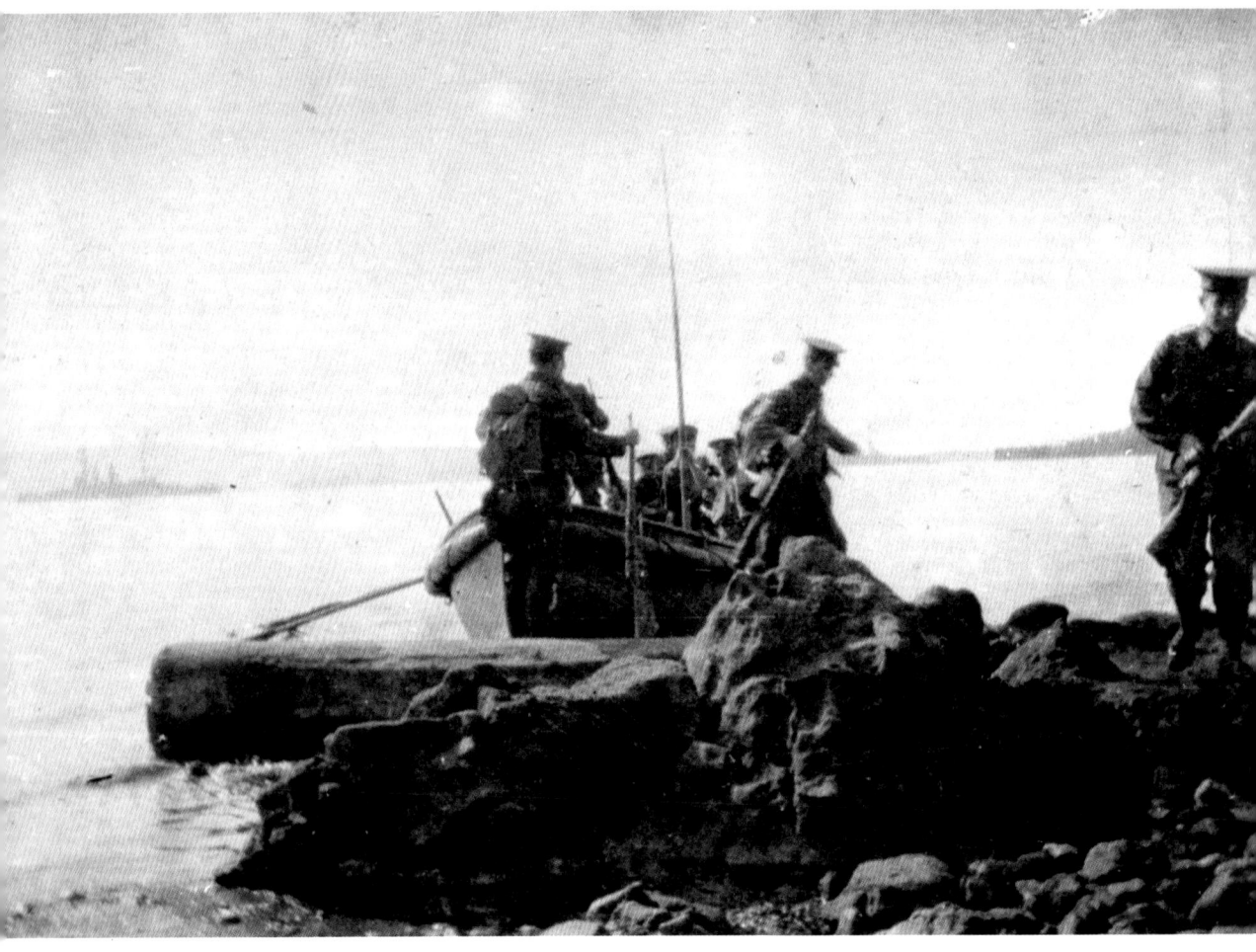

... nor death's cold flood, should fright us from the shore.

Isaac Watts

Soldiers stepping ashore at Gallipoli; they were among the
very few who managed to do so without getting their feet wet

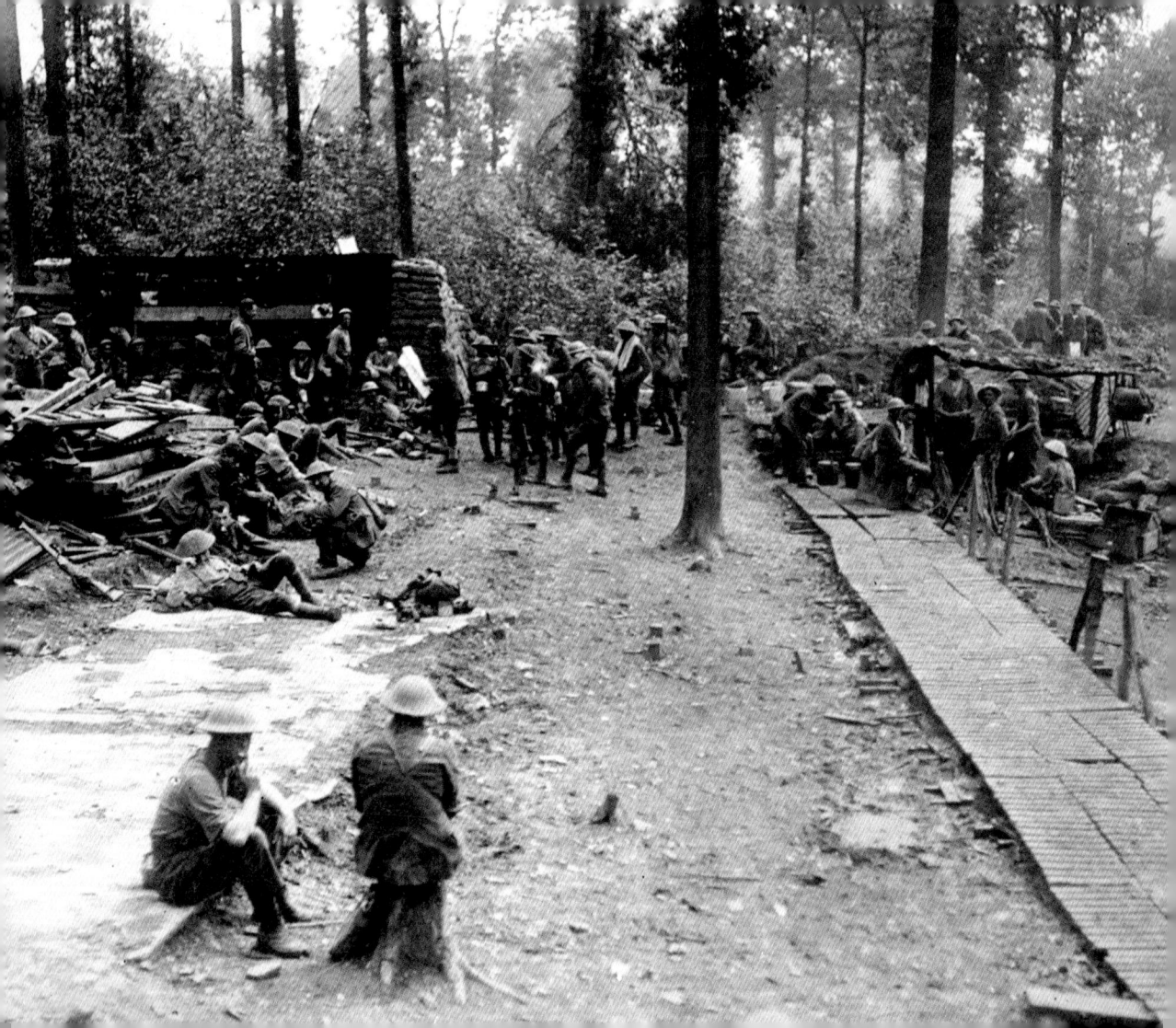

A hero is no braver than an ordinary man, but he is braver five minutes longer.

Ralph Waldo Emerson

New Zealand soldiers rest after close combat, Ploegsteert Wood ('Plug Street'), Belgium

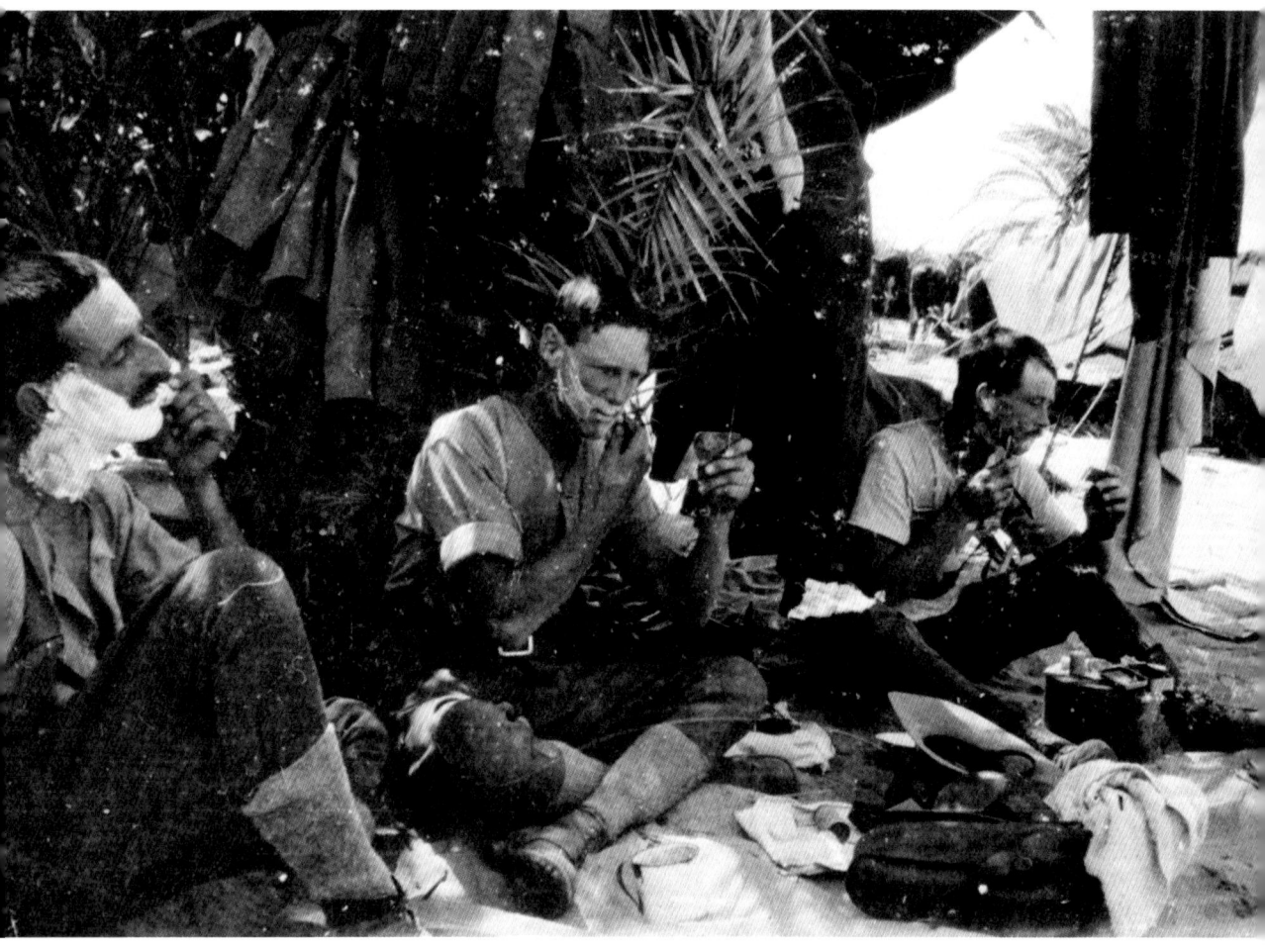

No evil can happen to a good man, either in life or after death.

Plato

Members of 11th Squadron, Auckland Mounted Rifles,
shaving under palm trees at Bir-el-Maler, Palestine

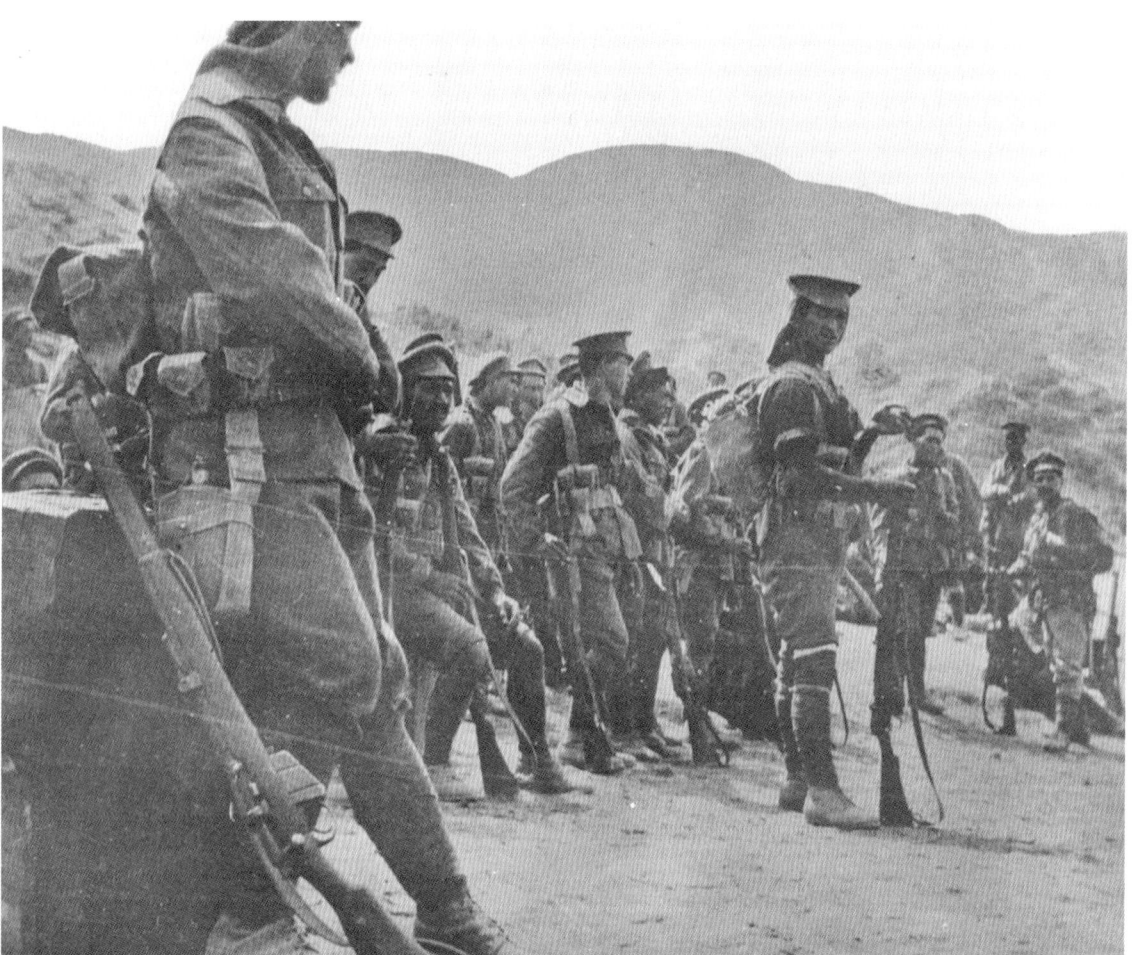

Soldiers usually win the battles and generals get the credit for them.

Napoleon Bonaparte

Maori infantrymen assemble before going into action

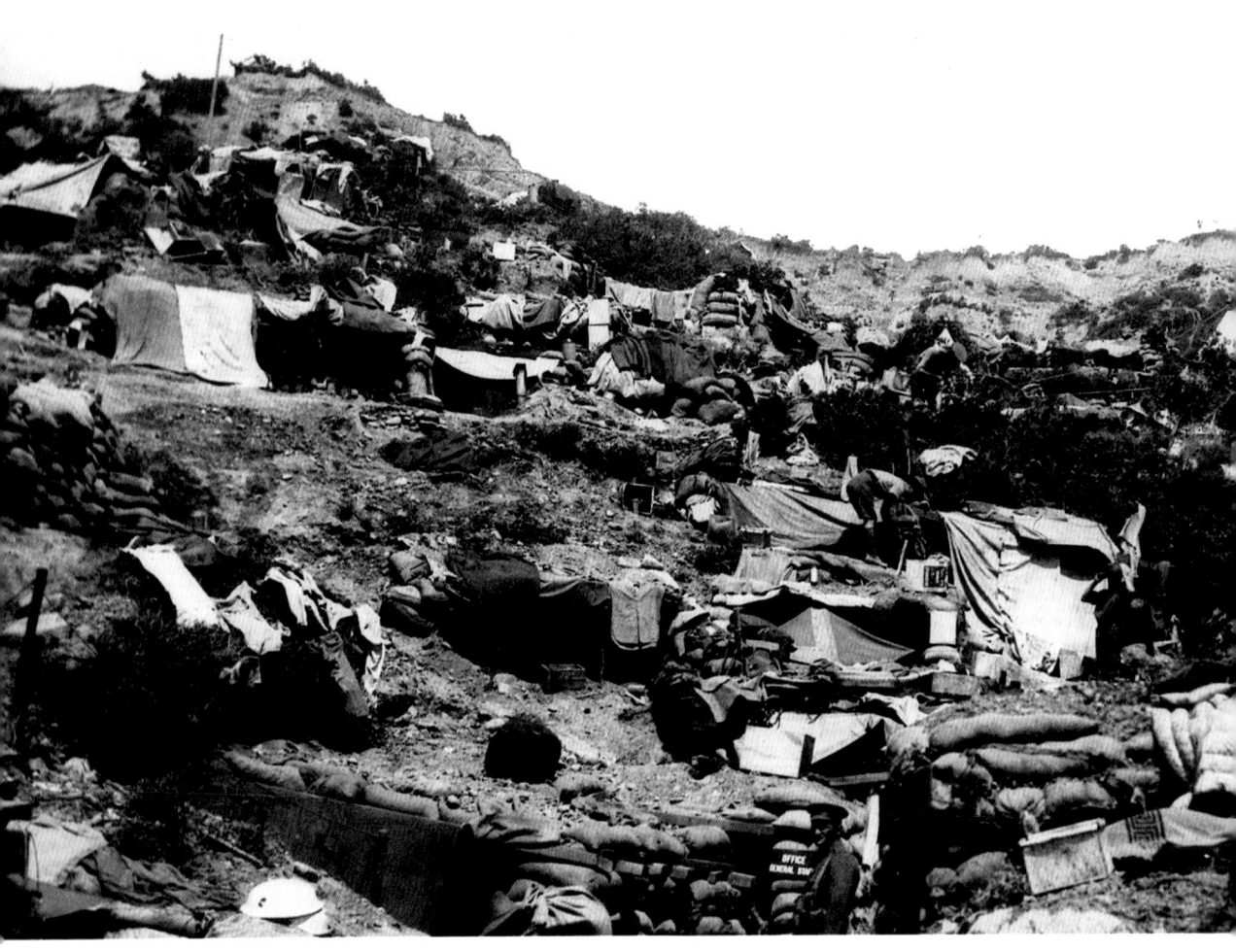

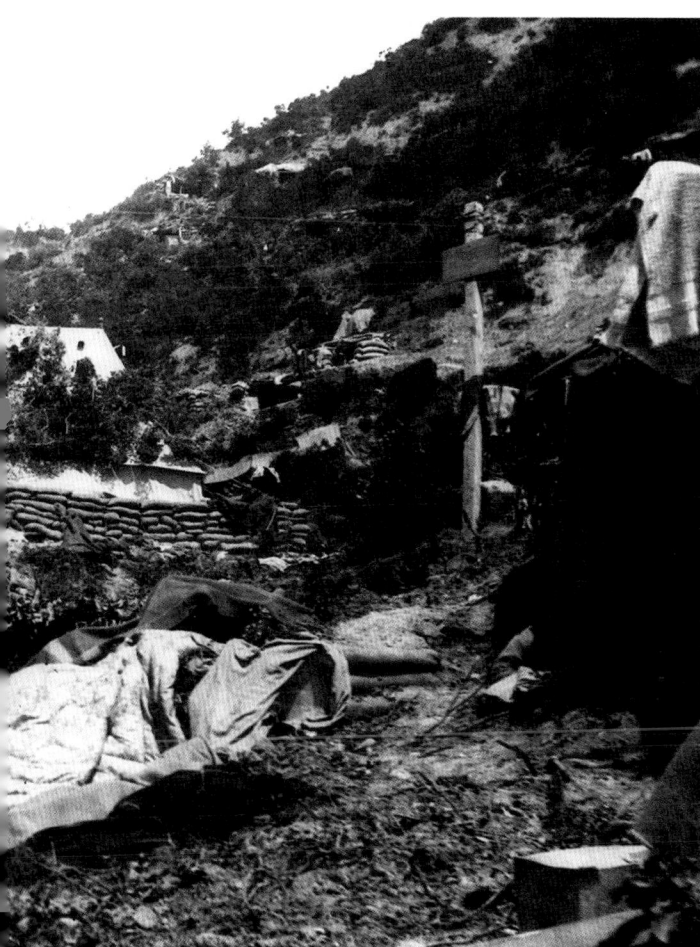

... it must have been a very fine and wonderful thing to have been one of that small Army that fought so gallantly for such a forlorn hope.

Vera Brittain

Bivouacs of the ANZAC base
at Headquarters Gully,
Anzac Cove, Gallipoli

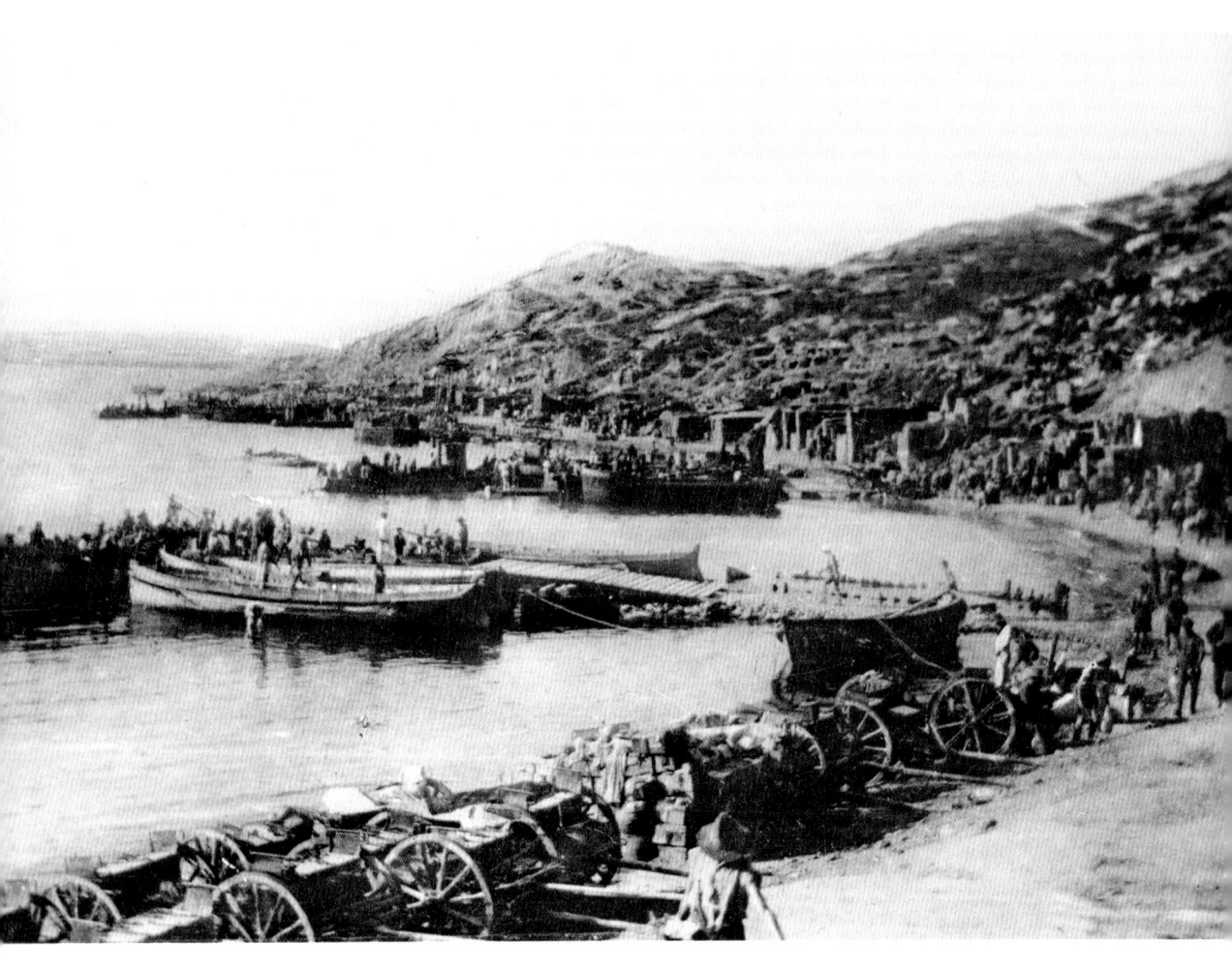

You can no more win a war than you can win an earthquake.

Jeannette Rankin

Men and matériel arriving at Anzac Beach, Gallipoli

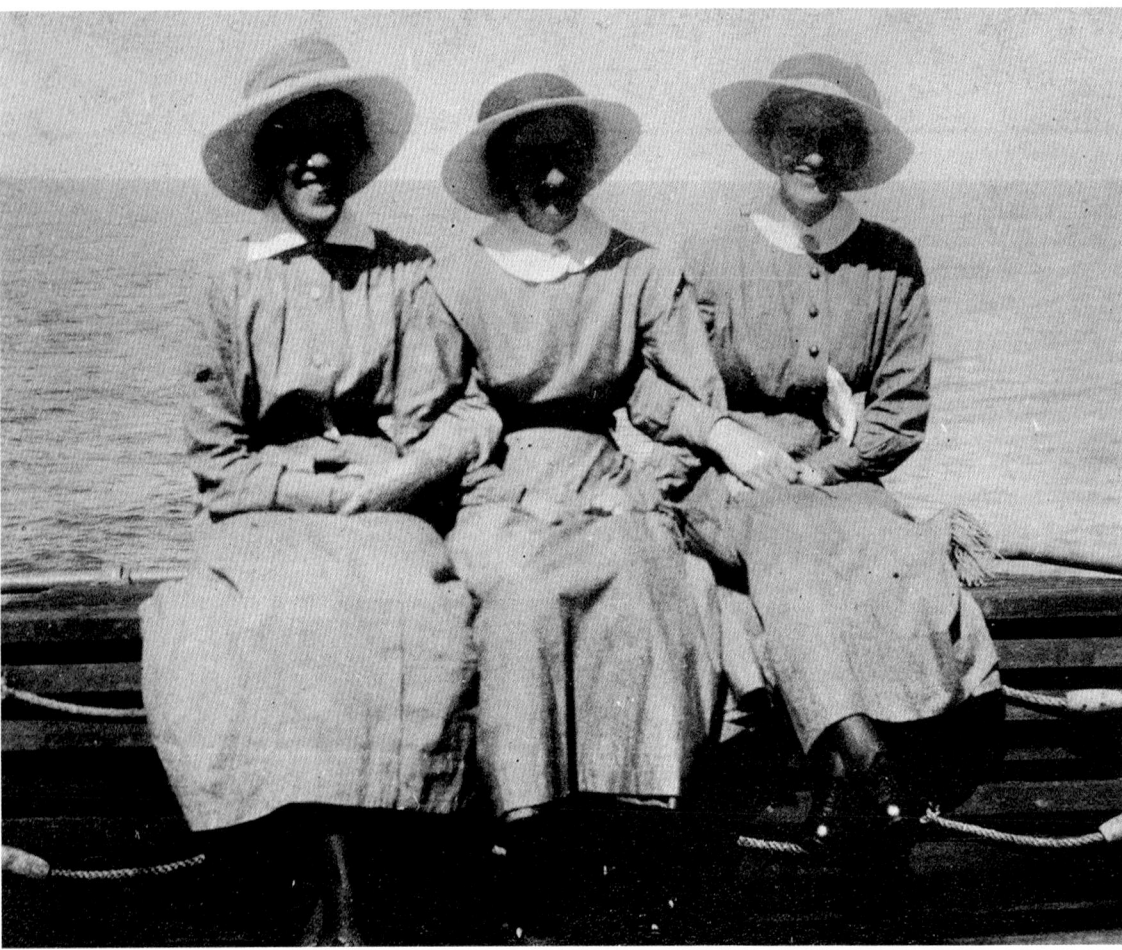

If there must be trouble let it be in my day, that my child may have peace.

Thomas Paine

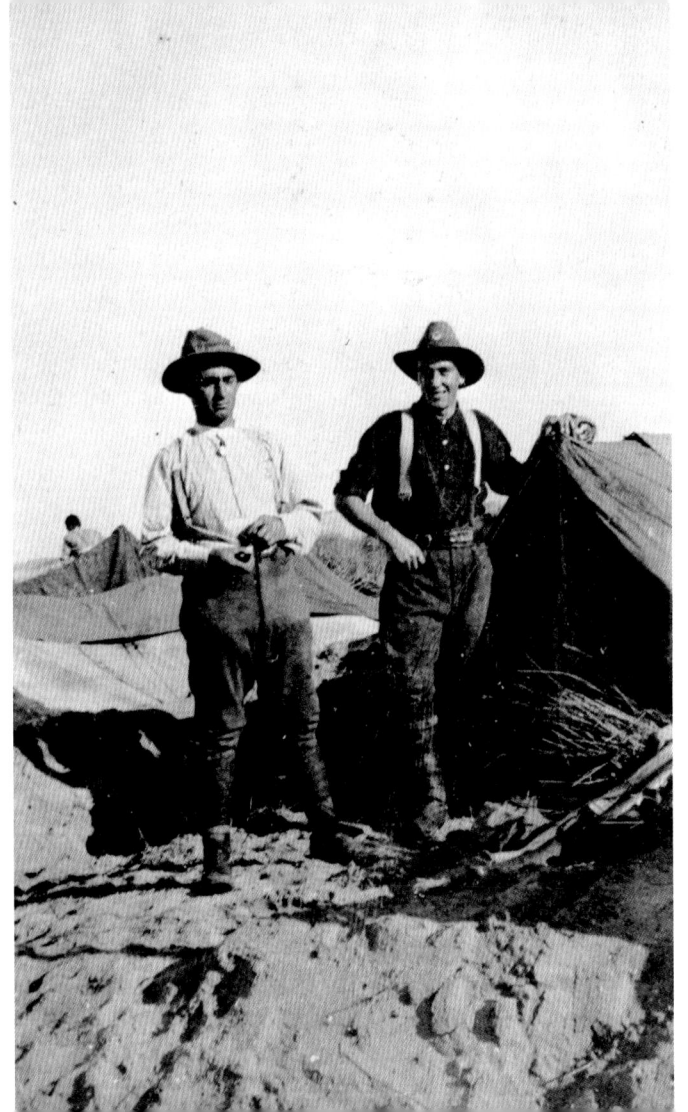

We were brothers all
In honour, as in one community,
Scholars and Gentlemen.

William Wordsworth

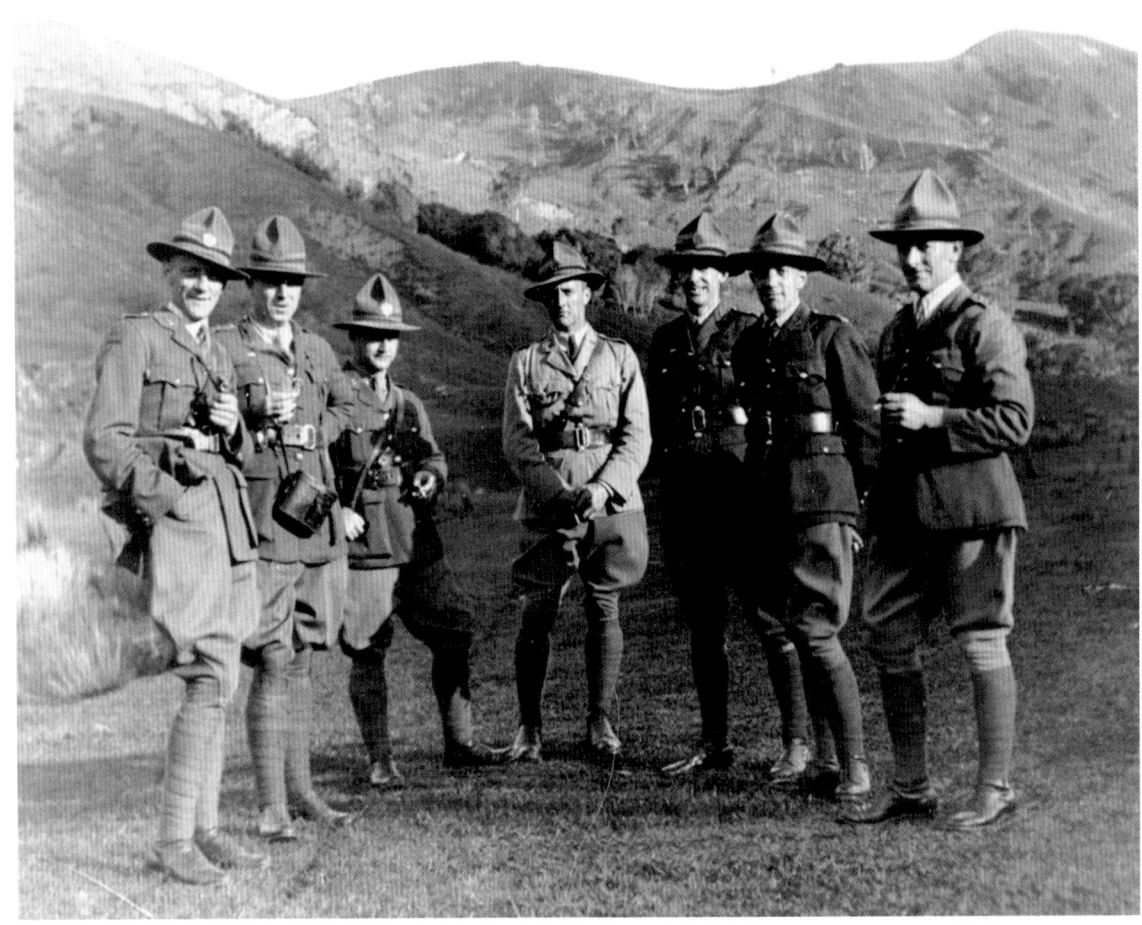

When a front line soldier overhears ...
General Staff officers conferring,
he has fallen back too far.

Anonymous

Away from the battles, a group of best-dressed officers poses for the camera

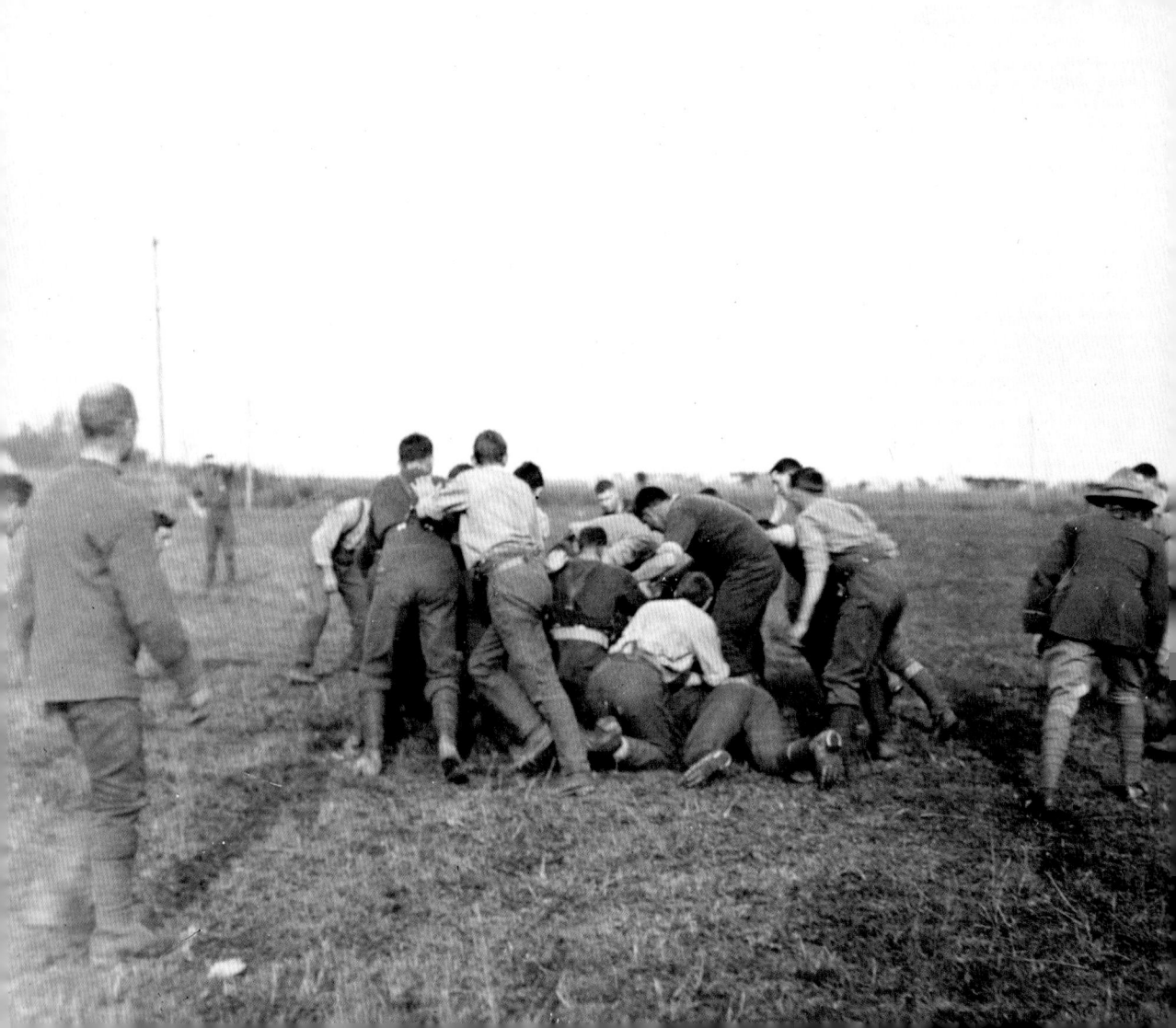

The referee has power to declare no side at any time, if the referee believes that play should not go on because it would be dangerous.

From *The Laws of Rugby Union Football*

New Zealand soldiers play an improvised rugby match in France, 1918

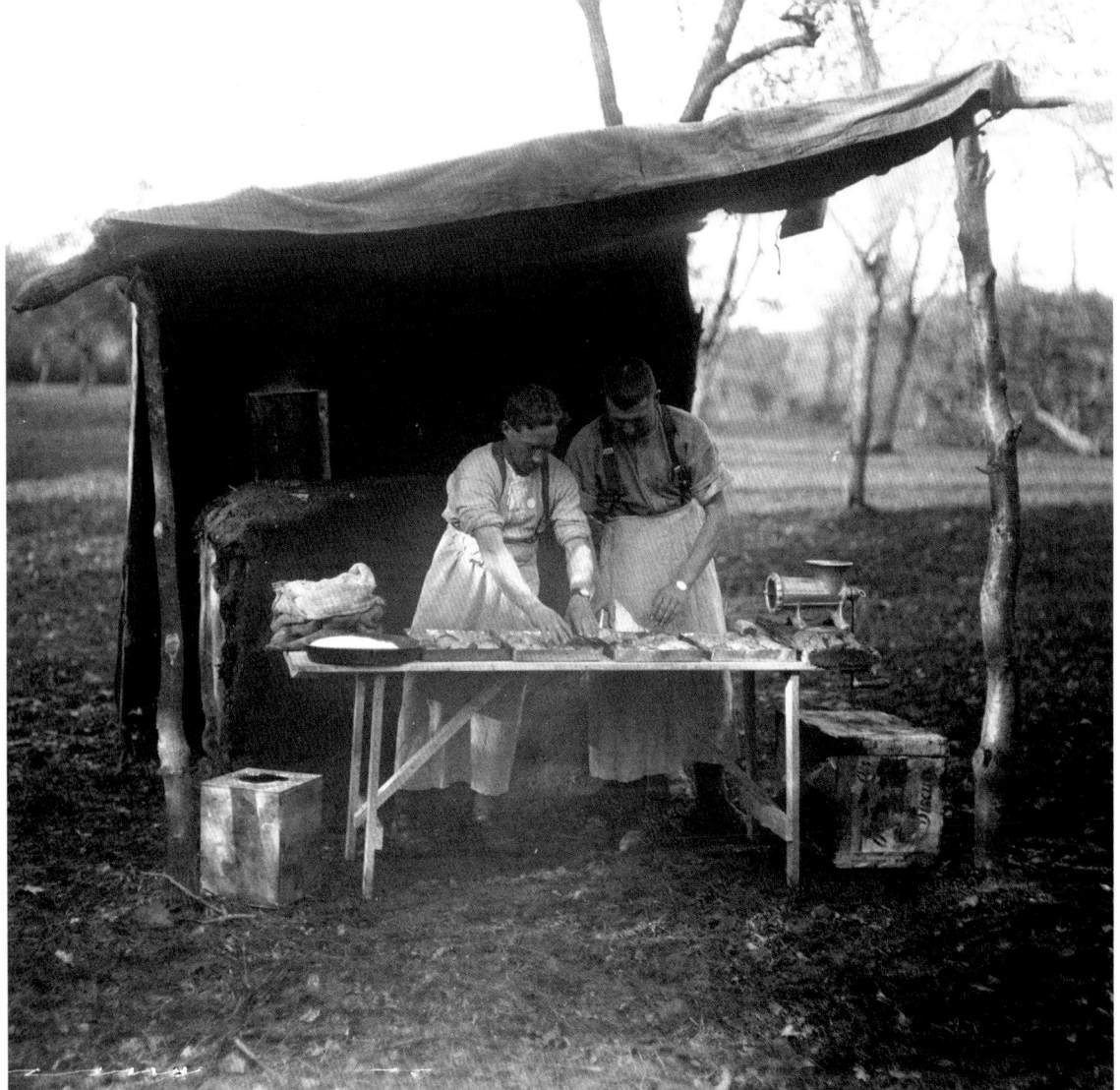

War is too serious a matter to entrust to military men.

Georges Clemenceau

Sausage rolls being cooked in a temporary field kitchen, France, 1917

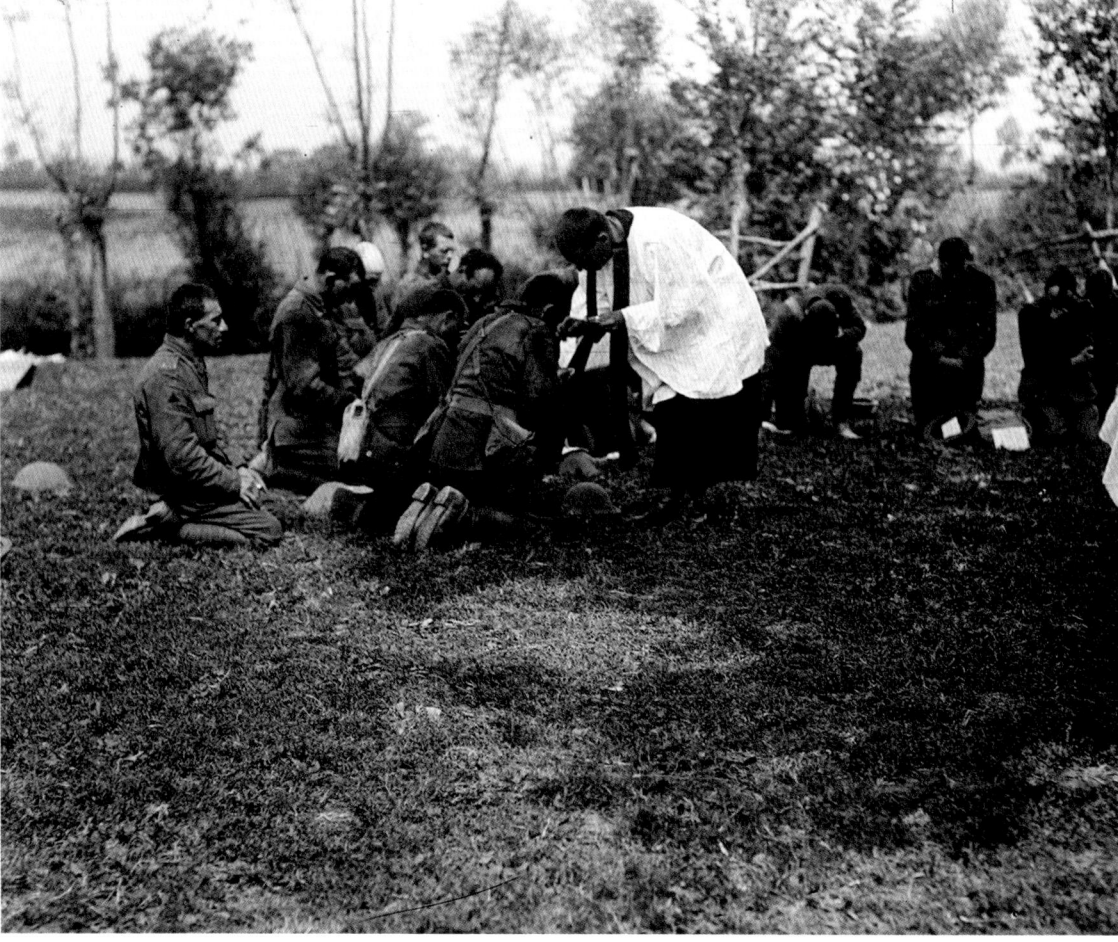

Gott mit uns

'God is with us' (slogan on German soldiers' uniform belt buckles)

Friend or foe, both sides worshipped the same God.
A New Zealand chaplain celebrates holy communion in Belgium

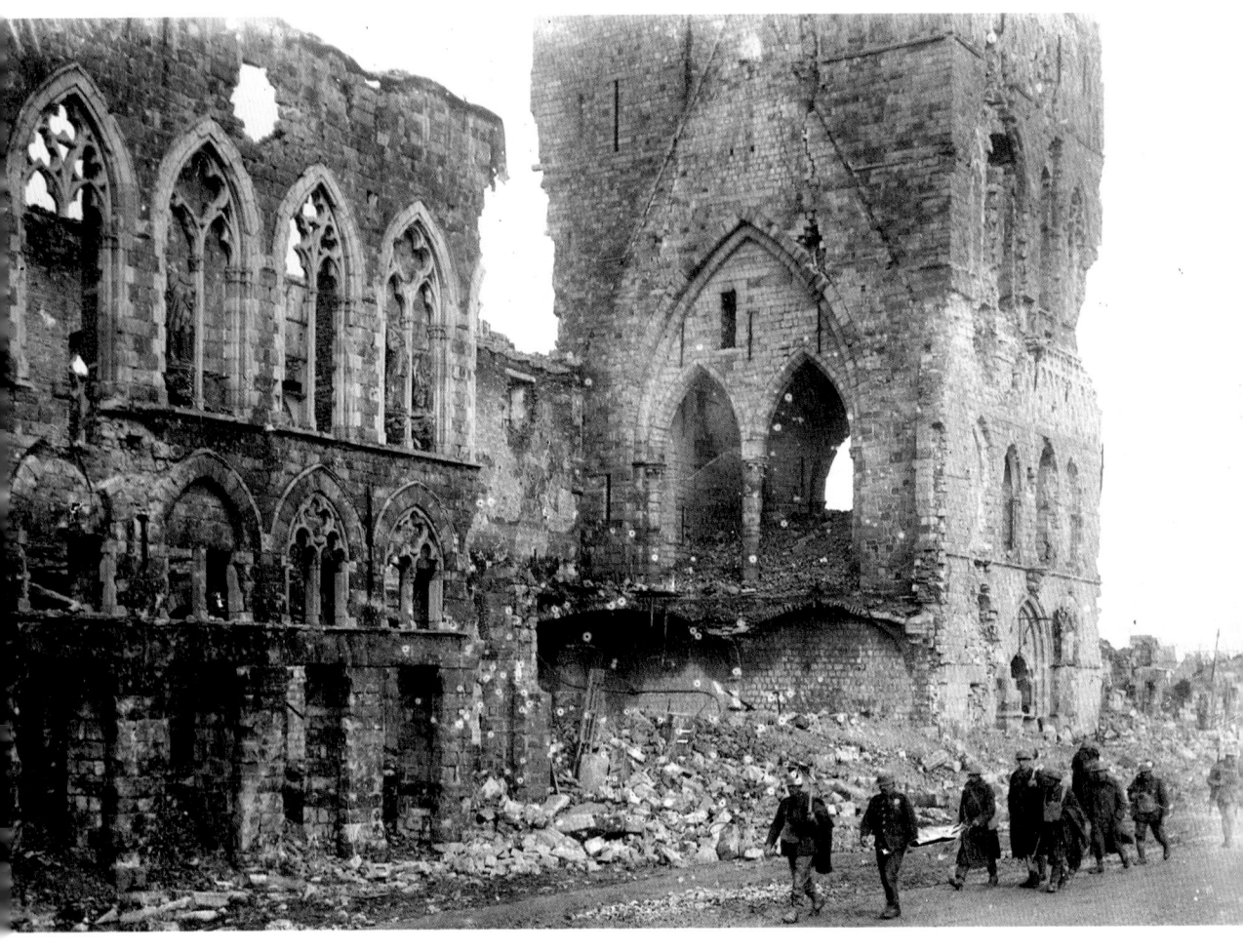

There are some defeats more triumphant than victories.

Michel de Montaigne

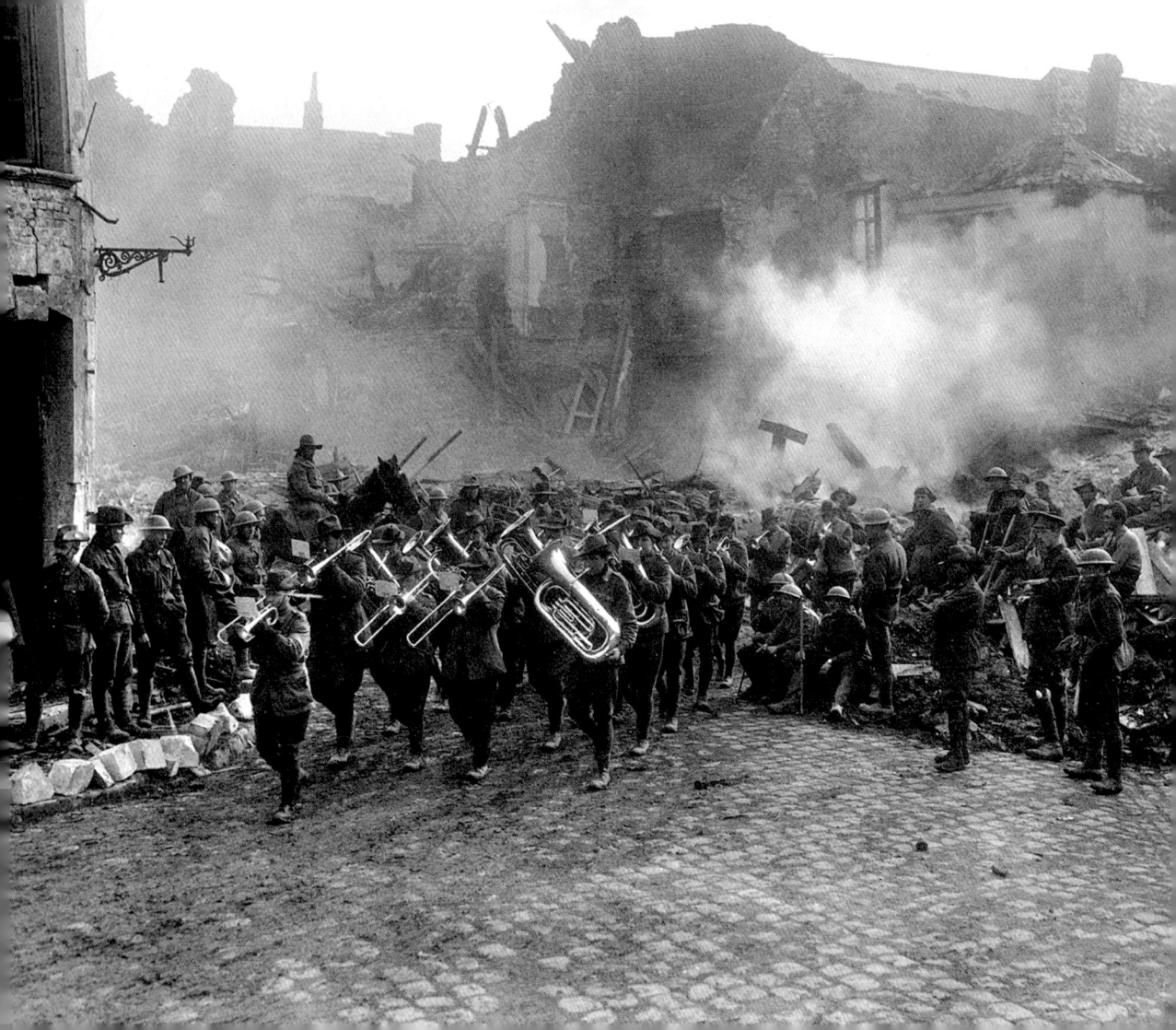

We learn from history that we learn nothing from history.

George Bernard Shaw

With 19 months of war still remaining, the band of the 5th Australian Infantry Brigade passes through the ruined Grande Place of Bapaume, France, playing the 'Victoria March'

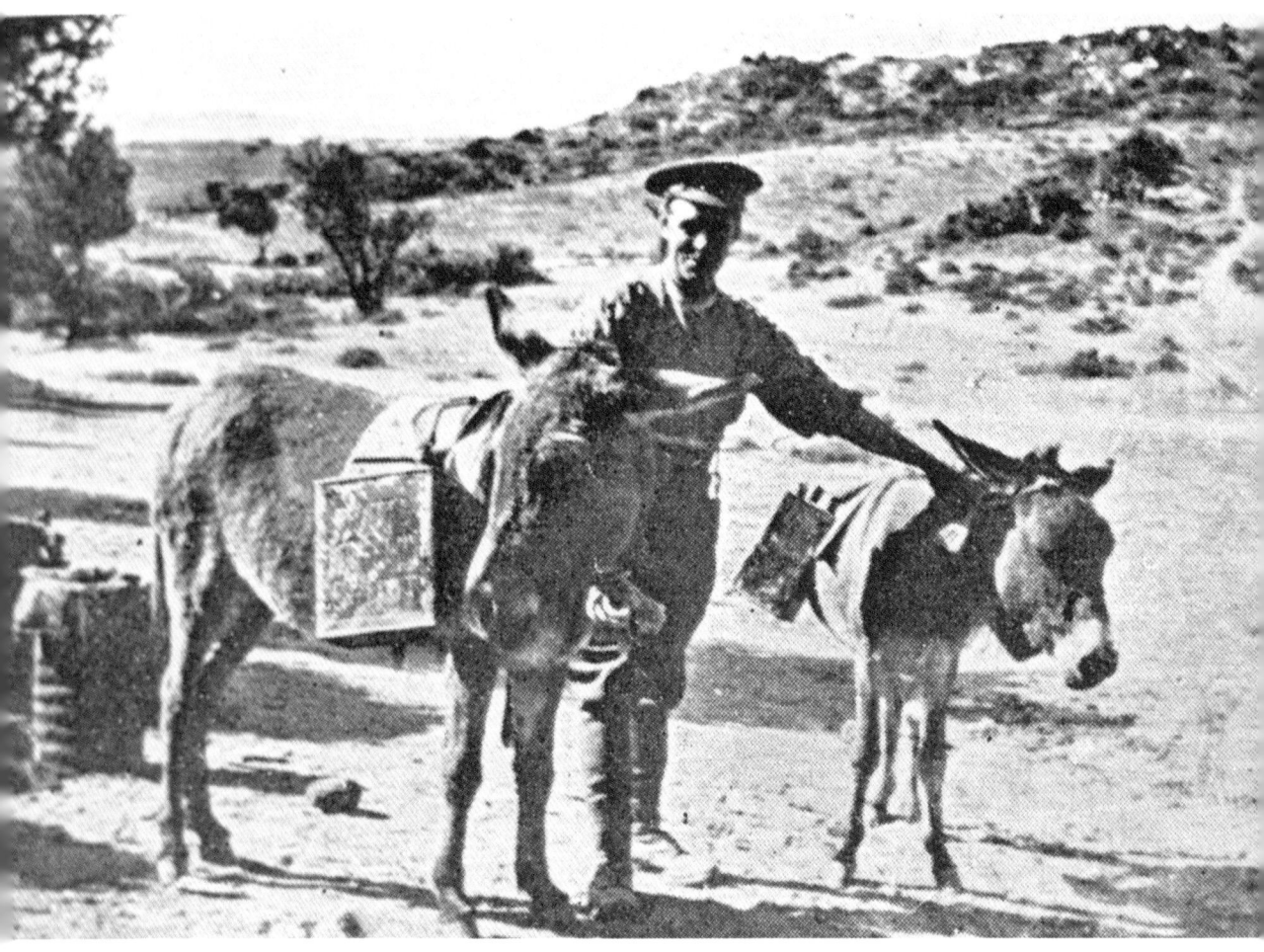

Courage is doing what you're afraid to do.
There can be no courage unless you're scared.

Eddie Rickenbacker

Some of war's most courageous men are those who supply the front.
Here a mule driver performs the thankless, dangerous,
repetitive task of bringing water to a howitzer battery

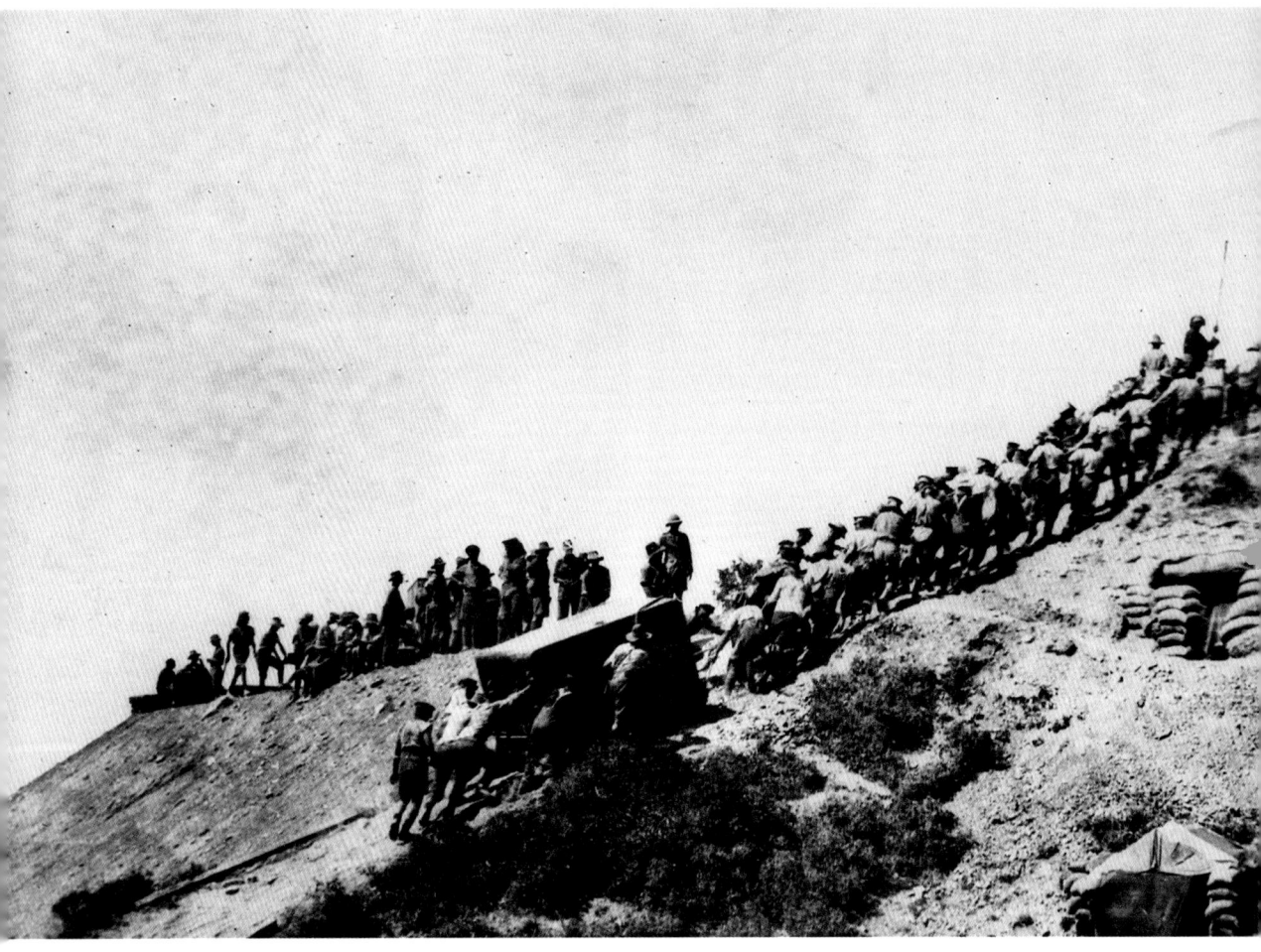

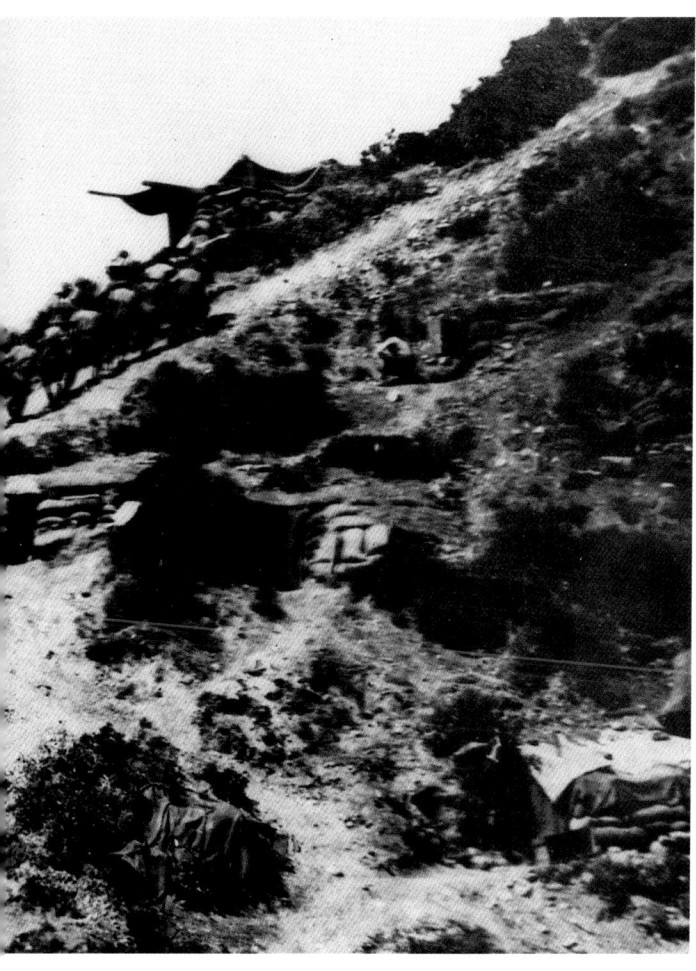

History is indeed little more than the register of the crimes, follies and misfortunes of mankind.

Edward Gibbon

Maori and Australian soldiers man-haul a water tank uphill from Anzac Cove, Gallipoli

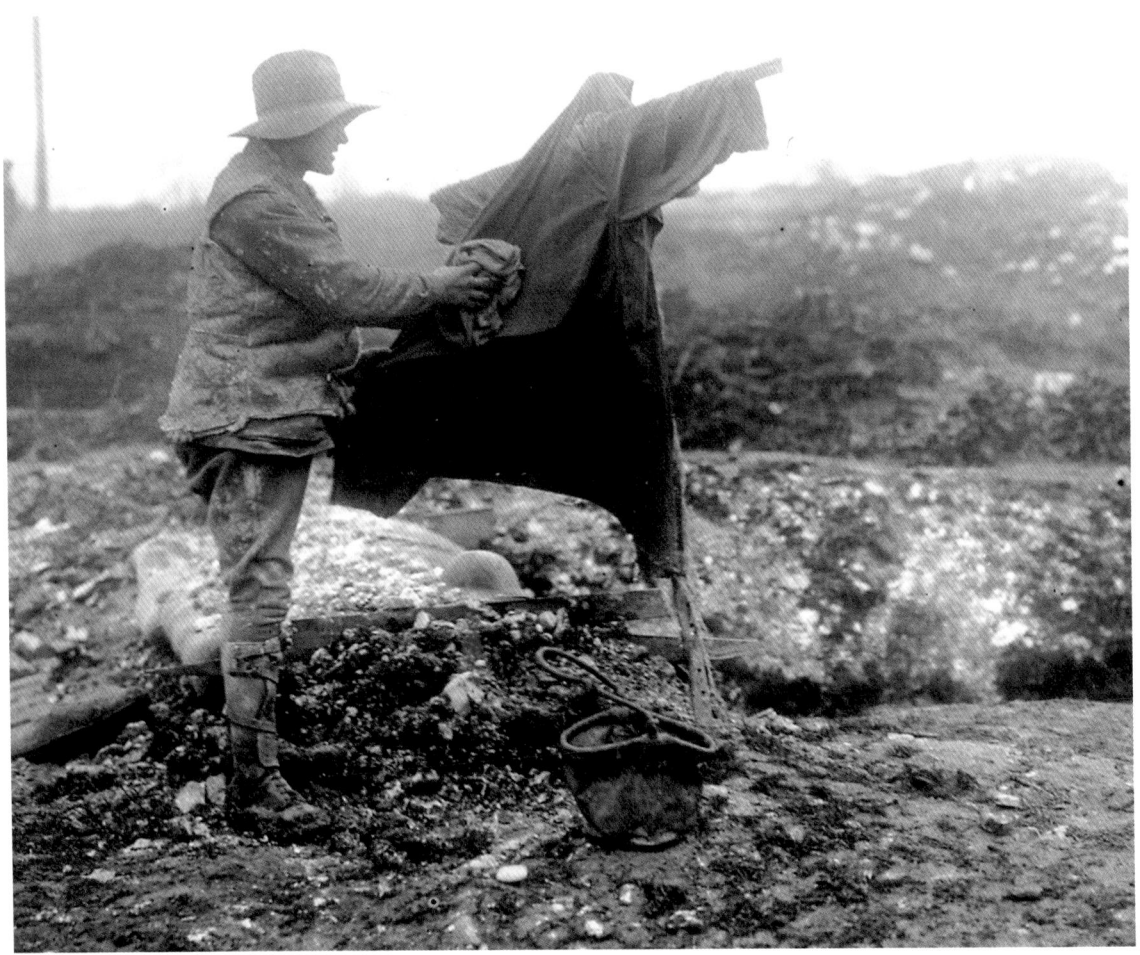

The soul of man is immortal and imperishable.

Plato

In a devastated landscape an ANZAC soldier tries to wash the filth
of the trenches off his shirt during a lull in fighting at the Somme

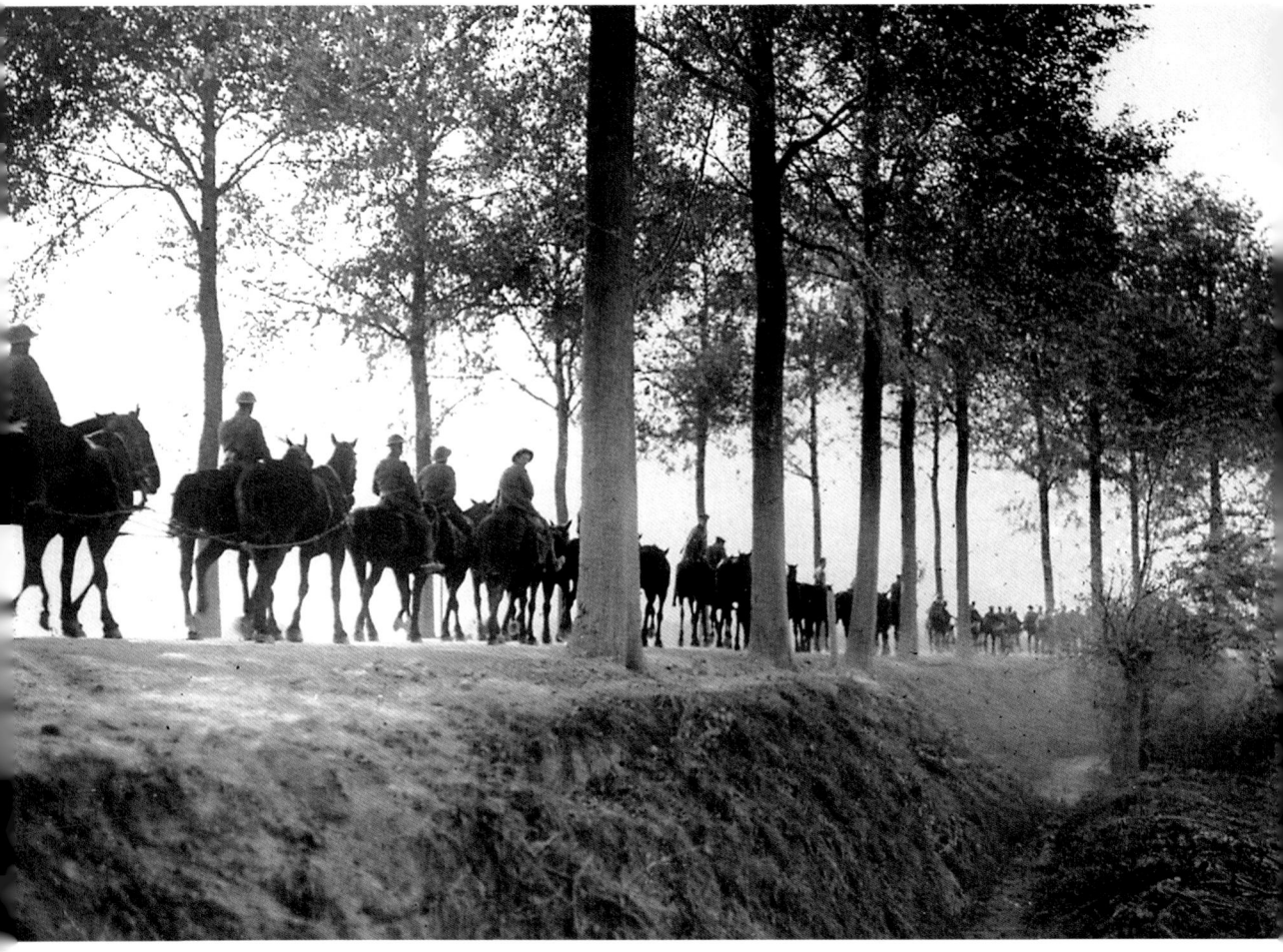

Farewell! thou art too dear for my possessing.

William Shakespeare

Mounted troops of the 1st ANZAC Corps moving along the tree-lined
Ypres road during the Battle of Polygon Wood, Passchendaele

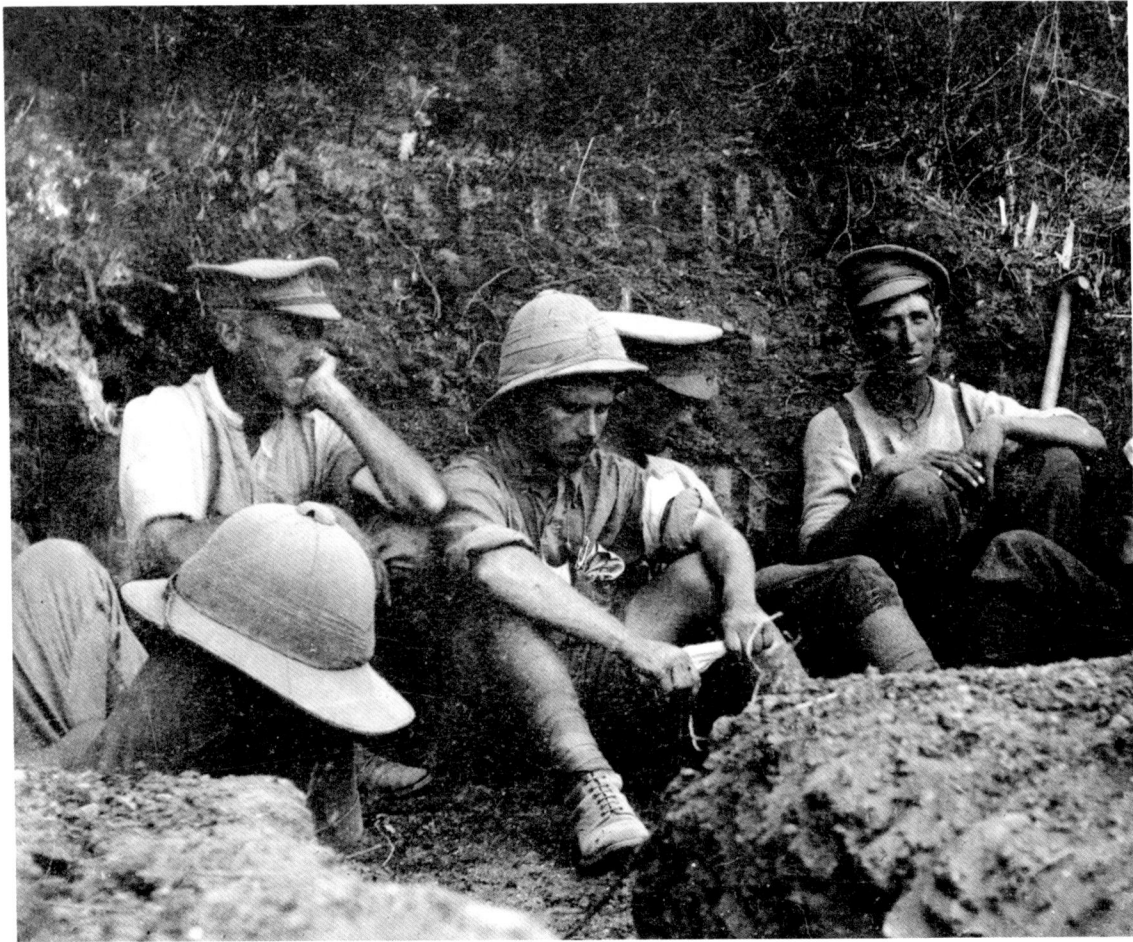

Guard your honor. Let your reputation fall where it will.
And outlive the bastards.

Lois McMaster Bujold

Soldiers wait for orders in a shallow trench shortly before the attack on Chunuk Bair, Gallipoli

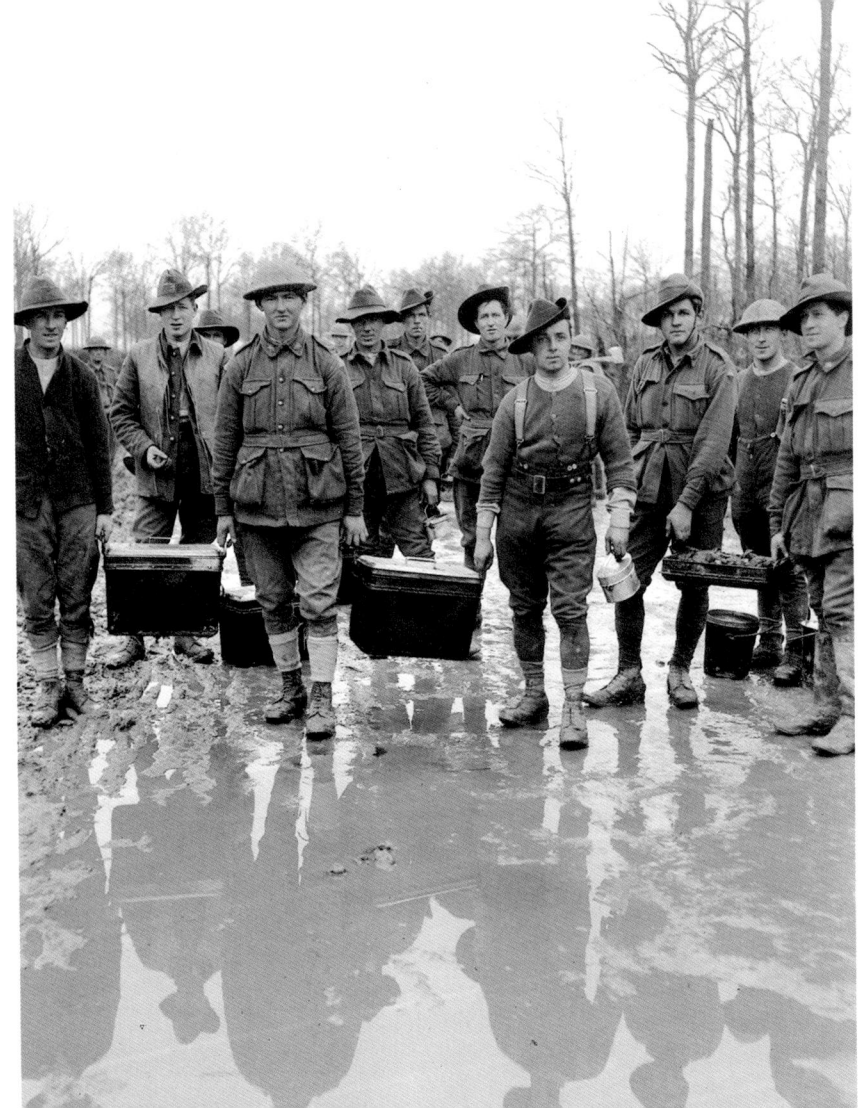

The greatest griefs are those we cause ourselves.

Sophocles

Orderlies carry hot soup to Australian reserve troops, Messines, Belgium

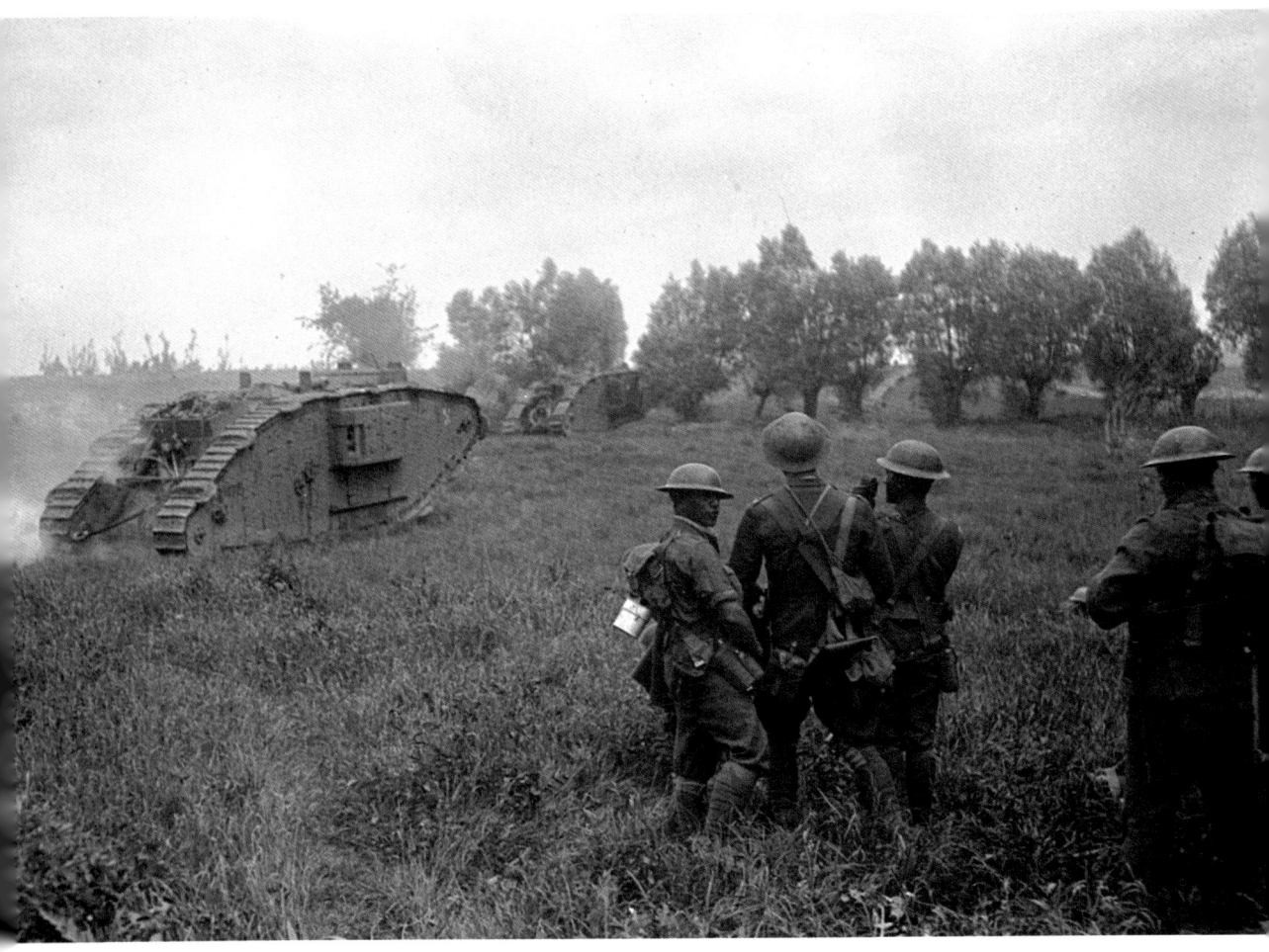

The profoundest truth of war is that the issue of battle is usually decided in the minds of the opposing commanders, not in the bodies of their men.

Basil Liddell Hart

Watched by New Zealanders, primitive tanks – first used in 1916 – move to attack Messines Ridge in 1917

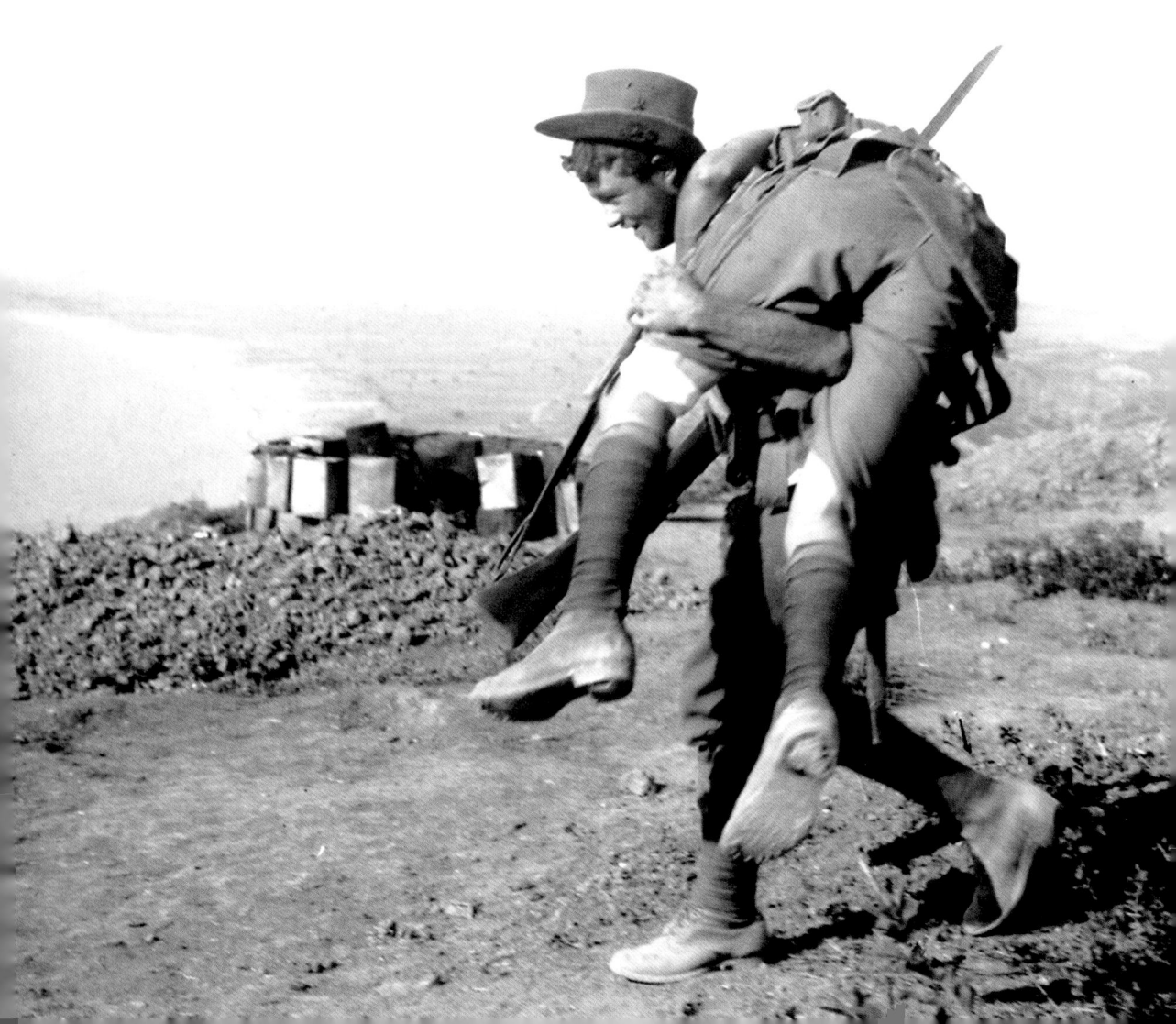

Anyone who has ever looked into the glazed eyes of a soldier dying on the battlefield will think hard before starting a war.

Otto von Bismarck

A wounded Australian is brought down for treatment from the deadly slopes of Gallipoli, 1915

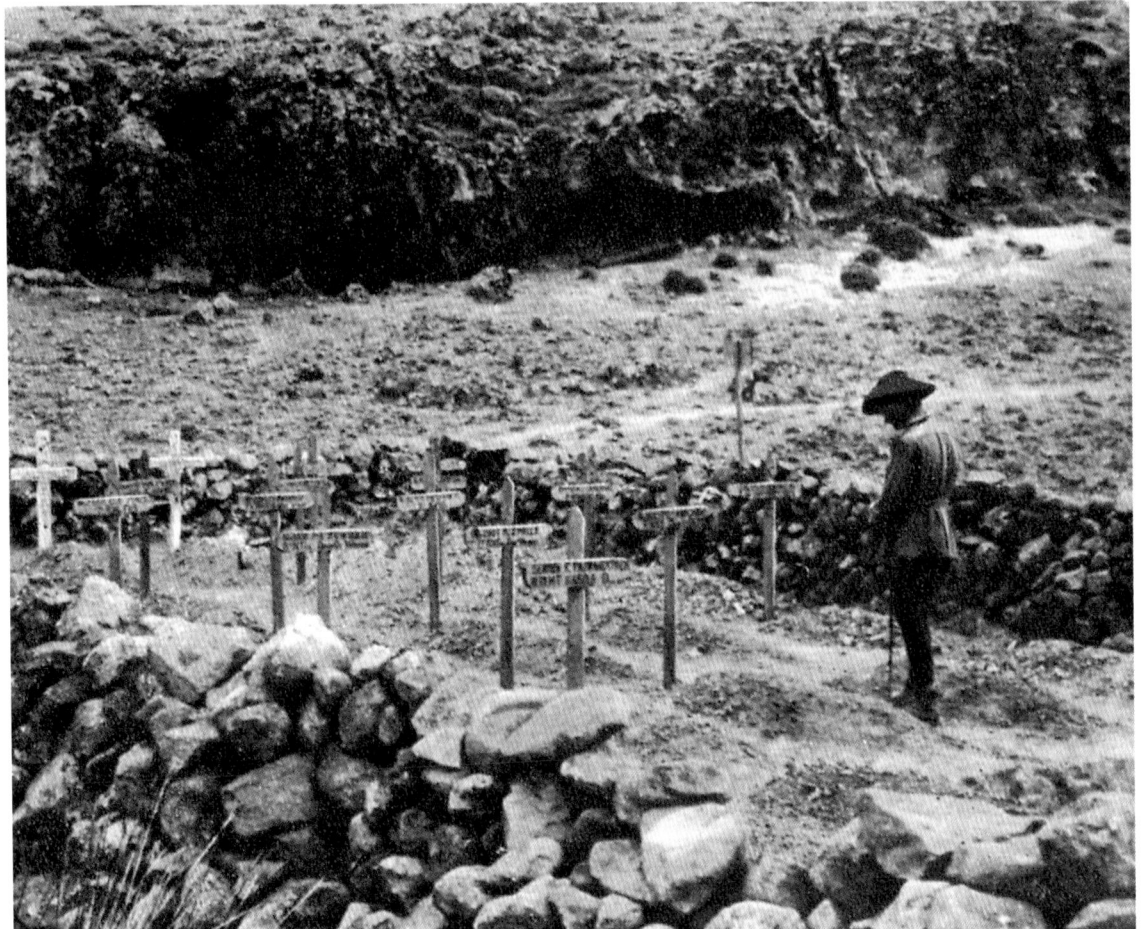

Anyone who has ever looked into the glazed eyes of a soldier dying on the battlefield will think hard before starting a war.

Otto von Bismarck

A wounded Australian is brought down for treatment from the deadly slopes of Gallipoli, 1915

IMPERIAL WAR MUSEUM (Q 13622)

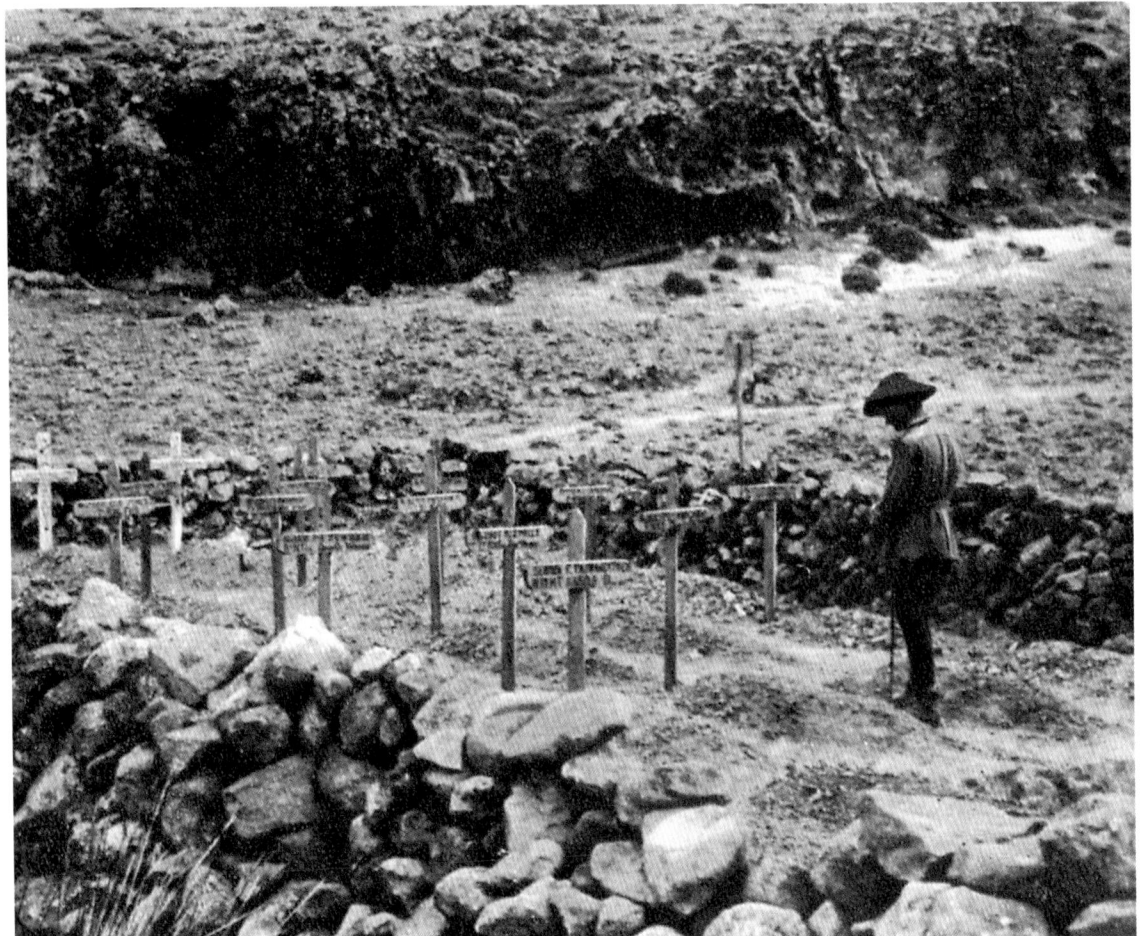

In peace the sons bury their fathers,
but in war the fathers bury their sons.

Croesus

An ANZAC farewell to comrades at Gallipoli
(from the *Silver Jubilee Book*, ODHAMS PRESS 1935)

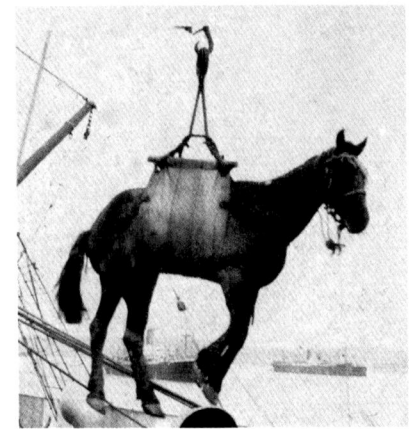

First published in 2005 by New Holland Publishers
Auckland • Sydney • London • Cape Town

218 Lake Road, Northcote, Auckland, New Zealand
14 Aquatic Drive, Frenchs Forest, NSW 2086, Australia
86–88 Edgware Road, London W2 2EA, United Kingdom
80 McKenzie Street, Cape Town 8001, South Africa

www.newhollandpublishers.co.nz

Copyright © 2005 in concept: Renée Lang
Renaissance Publishing
Copyright © 2005 New Holland Publishers (NZ) Ltd

ISBN: 1 86966 085 4

Compilation: Don Donovan
Design: Gina Hochstein

Colour reproduction by Microdot, Auckland, New Zealand
Printed by Star Standard Industries (Pte) Ltd, Singapore

Acknowledgements
Photographs on pp 8, 16, 66, 68, 76 reproduced with the permission
of the Trustees of the Imperial War Museum, London